The Paralympic Games Explained

The Paralympic Games is the second largest multi-sport festival on earth and an event which poses profound and challenging questions about the nature of sport, disability and society. *The Paralympic Games Explained* is the first complete introduction to the Paralympic phenomenon, exploring every key aspect and issue, from the history and development of the Paralympic movement to the economic and social impact of the contemporary Games.

The book introduces the three most important theoretical models of disability (medical, social and bio-social), to enable the reader to fully understand the Paralympics in the context of wider discussions of disability in society. It also offers a straightforward explanation of the importance of language and terminology in shaping our understanding of disability and disability sport. Including international examples and comparative material throughout, the book offers detailed and broad-ranging discussion of key issues such as:

- How societal attitudes influence disability sport
- The governance of Paralympic and elite disability sport
- The relationship between the Paralympics and the Olympics
- Drugs and technology in disability sport
- Classification in disability sport

Containing useful features throughout, such as review questions, study activities, web links and guides to further reading, *The Paralympic Games Explained* is the most accessible, comprehensive and thoughtful guide to the Paralympics currently available. It is essential reading for all students with an interest in disability sport, sporting mega-events, the politics of sport, or disability in society.

Ian Brittain has formerly been an Executive Board member of the International Stoke Mandeville Wheelchair Sports Federation and was the Sports Co-ordinator for the International Wheelchair and Amputee Sports Federation World Games in Rio de Janiero. He has attended the last three Summer Paralympic Games in Sydney, Athens and Beijing. His research focuses upon sociological, historical and sports management aspects of Paralympic and disability sport.

The Paralympic Games Explained

Withdrawn/ABCL

Ian Brittain

Routledge
Taylor & Francis Group

LONDON AND NEW YORK

First published 2010
by Routledge
2 Park Square, Milton Park, Abingdon, Oxon, OX14 4RN

Simultaneously published in the USA and Canada
by Routledge
711 Third Avenue, New York, NY 10017

Routledge is an imprint of the Taylor & Francis Group, an Informa business

© 2010 Ian Brittain

Typeset in Sabon by
HWA Text and Data Management, London

British Library Cataloguing in Publication Data
A catalogue record for this book is available from the British Library

Library of Congress Cataloging-in-Publication Data
Brittain, Ian.
   The Paralympic Games Explained / Ian Brittain
      p. cm.
   Includes bibliographical references and index.
   1. Paralympics. 2. Sports for people with disabilities. I. Title.
   GV722.5.P37B75 2010
   796.04´56-dc22   2009008287

ISBN13: 978-0-415-47658-4 (hbk)
ISBN13: 978-0-415-47659-1 (pbk)
ISBN13: 978-0-203-88556-7 (ebk)

ISBN10: 0-415-47658-5 (hbk)
ISBN10: 0-415-47659-3 (pbk)
ISBN10: 0-203-88556-2 (ebk)

Contents

Illustrations

Plates

Figures

Tables

Foreword

On behalf of the International Paralympic Committee (IPC), I welcome this publication to the Paralympic library of knowledge and information. *The Paralympic Games Explained* provides a clear picture of the Paralympic Movement and the many distinct features that might not yet be of general knowledge.

In my role as President of the IPC, I was a part of the extensive preparation for the Beijing 2008 Paralympic Games. The Games last year broke numerous records that when combined, show the dramatic increase in development that Paralympic sport has undergone recently. Beijing saw almost 4,000 athletes from a total of 146 different countries compete in the Chinese capital. Together, their strong performances set 279 new world records, as well as 339 new Paralympic records. These records were avidly watched by spectators and television audiences from all over the world.

The Beijing Paralympic Games found the largest television audience in Paralympic history. More than 3.8 billion people in 38 monitored countries watched the athletes compete during more than 1,800 hours of broadcast time. The highest live audience was registered in China for the Closing Ceremony on 17 September, with 51 million viewers.

Together the numbers create a new level of awareness concerning not only the Paralympic Games, but Paralympic athletes and their high performance capability.

This publication explains the Movement behind the Paralympics, and the many aspects that are connected to its success. Each chapter contains its own furthering of detail in the history and future of the Paralympic Games. Background can be learnt in 'History and development of the Paralympic Games' and 'The governance of Paralympic sport', while topics relevant today can be dissected in 'The broader social issues of disability within society and their impact on sports participation'.

As you read *The Paralympic Games Explained*, I hope you are able to come away with information that will make you a lifelong fan of Paralympic Sport. You will find that the athletes achieve their sporting excellence and consequently inspire and excite your world.

Sir Philip Craven, MBE
President – International Paralympic Committee

Acknowledgements

The information for this book was drawn from a wide range of sources. Numerous individuals have assisted in a variety of ways, each providing a small piece of the jigsaw that went to make up this book. However, I would like to give special thanks to the following:

All my friends and contacts working at the International Paralympic Committee and the International Olympic Committee who answered countless questions and provided resource material for the book.

Sean Gammon for patiently reading each chapter, despite an already heavy workload, and giving me a lecturer's perspective on the content.

My friend Oriel Martinez, a member of the International Paralympic Committee Therapeutic Use Exemption Committee for providing me with data and answering many questions with regard to anti-doping.

All my friends and contacts working in disability sport around the world who provided material and commented upon drafts of the 'Snapshots' included in Chapter nine, especially Dr Jagdish Maharaj, Peter Downs and Neil Wilford.

Thank you one and all!

Acronyms

AHSN	Athletes with High Support Needs
APC	Australian Paralympic Committee
ASEAN	Association of South East Asian Nations
BLESMA	British Limbless Ex-Servicemen's Association
BOCOG	Beijing Organising Committee of the Olympic Games
CAS	Court of Arbitration for Sport
CDPF	Chinese Disabled Peoples Federation
CP-ISRA	Cerebal Palsied International Sports and Recreation Association
CISS	Comité International des Sports des Sourds
CNVLD	Cambodian National Volleyball League (Disabled)
DQS	Delegation Quota System
EHRC	Equality and Human Rights Commission
FEI	Fédération Equestre Internationale
FISA	Fédération Internationale des Sociétés d'Aviron
FITA	Fédération Internationale Tir a l'Arc
FINA	Fédération Internationale de Natation
HI	Handicap-International
IAAF	International Assocation of Athletics Federations
IBD	International Bowls for the Disabled
IBSA	International Blind Sports Association
ICC	International Co-ordinating Committee
IFDS	International Federation for Disabled Sailing
INAS-FID	International Sports Federation for People with an Intellectual Disability
INAS-FMH	International Association of Sports for Persons with a Mental Handicap
IOC	International Olympic Committee
IPC	International Paralympic Committee
IPSF	International Paralympic Sports Federation
IOSD	International Organisations for Sport for the Disabled
ISMGF	International Stoke Mandeville Games Federation

ISMWSF	International Stoke Mandeville Wheelchair Sports Federation
ISOD	International Sports Organisation for the Disabled
IWAS	International Wheelchair and Amputee Sports Federation
NOC	National Olympic Committee
NOSD	National Organisation for Sport for the Disabled
NPC	National Paralympic Committee
NWAA	National Wheelchair Athletic Association
OCOG	Organising Committee of the Olympic Games
PPP	Paralympic Preparation Program
TUE	Therapeutic Use Exemption
UCI	Union Cycliste Internationale
UKSA	UK Sports Association for People with Learning Diffiiculties
USOC	United States Olympic Committee
WADA	World Anti-Doping Agency
WCF	World Curling Federation
WOVD	World Organisation Volleyball for the Disabled
ZDVO	Zahal Disabled Veterans Organisation

Introduction

Paralympic and disability sport is a seriously under researched area with a dearth of academic material. Disability issues impact upon all areas of life. As such, any piece of research that has been carried out in the area of non-disabled sport can also be applied to Paralympic and disability sport, with numerous extra issues to consider on top that make the outcomes both interesting, informative and useful. There is already an emerging area of research entitled Olympic studies; however, this still leaves a gaping hole in the research agenda. Despite the fact that there is now a strong working link between the International Olympic Committee (IOC) and the International Paralympic Committee (IPC) most Olympic studies courses and researchers pay scant attention to the Paralympic Games. The Paralympic Games are the jewel in the crown of the Paralympic Movement just as the Olympic Games are for the Olympic Movement and are an almost untouched area for any researcher wishing to instigate a completely new area for study.

This lack of any perceived interest in Paralympic and disability sport is, for disabled people, simply a further affirmation of their exclusion from the rest of society based upon non-disabled perceptions of their abilities, which for the most part are unfounded. The aim of this book, therefore, is to provide information and data regarding the Paralympic Games that will hopefully provoke interest and further research in this fascinating area of sport. The Paralympic Games are a modern day sporting phenomenon that have grown from a small archery demonstration event sixty-one years ago to become the second largest multi-sport festival on the planet after the Olympic Games. Despite this there are still many misunderstandings and misconceptions regarding both the Paralympic Games and disability sport in general. Part of the reason for these misunderstandings and misconceptions is the aforementioned dearth of academic research and introductory texts regarding these Games and the issues that surround them. Given this fact the main purpose of this book is to clear up many of these misunderstandings by providing a clear and accessible text that clearly explains how the Paralympic Games have developed and the kinds of issues both their organisers and the athletes that compete in them have had to overcome to reach the stage they are at today.

Plate 0.1 Archery, the very first competitive sport for athletes with disabilities, has developed a long way since the first competition on 29 July 1948

The structure of the book

The first two chapters trace the development of the Paralympic Games from their inception as an archery demonstration event at Stoke Mandeville Hospital, UK to the second largest multi-sport festival on the planet after the Olympic Games. They highlight the visionary nature of the Games founder, Sir Ludwig Guttmann, and the methods he used to gain acceptance of, and media coverage for, the early Stoke Mandeville Games. Guttmann constantly drew parallels between the Stoke Mandeville Games and the Olympics and so the development and outcomes of the relationship between the two movements and the impact this has had on the Paralympic Games in recent times are outlined. This is followed in Chapter 3 by a discussion of the development of the modern day organisational structure for international disability sport and the Paralympic Games with a description of who the main organisations are and what their roles are within the Paralympic Movement.

The aim of the chapter on disability and the body is to introduce the reader to the three models of disability (medical, social and bio-social) that exist to try and explain many of the problems that disabled people face in their day-to-day lives. This will, hopefully, give the reader a better understanding of many of the issues that arise in the following chapters. The chapter will explain how the social model was developed by disability activists to help fight the dominant medicalised understanding of disability and how the medical view of disability impacts upon people's perceptions of disability and disability sport. It concludes by outlining the importance of language in this understanding and how the socially constructed and value-laden meanings attached to words such as 'disabled' and 'athlete' mean that when the words are put together to form 'disabled athlete' for many people there is an immediate and fundamental contradiction. This then immediately colours people's perceptions of the validity of sport for the disabled as 'real' sport.

Chapter 5 explores how societal attitudes to disability and disability sport can impact upon the opportunities for people with disabilities to become involved in sport and progress to the highest levels. The perceptions of disability embedded in the medical model discourse play a major part in structuring the perceptions that people hold and the ways in which they interact in relation to people with disabilities. As a result disability often becomes the dominant feature of their social identity as perceived by those around them. As a consequence of these views, and experiences of social interaction, disability, for people with disabilities, can also become the dominant feature of their own self-perception and self-image. Therefore, because disability is seen as a negative, and connected to incapability, all of the above mentioned factors may combine to inhibit involvement in sporting activities. This chapter will highlight many of the issues, both psychological and tangible, that can flow from this and act as barriers to disabled people becoming involved in and reaching the very highest levels of their chosen sport.

With the growth in importance of and participation in the Paralympic Games there has been a steady increase in media coverage. However, such coverage can vary greatly from country to country and the nature of the coverage can often serve to reinforce negative stereotypes of disability and disability sport. In order to try and overcome this the International Paralympic Committee (IPC) launched an internet based television station in 2006 in order to try and overcome some of these issues and provide access in countries with no television coverage. In addition, media coverage can also impact upon the ability of the International Paralympic Committee to effectively and successfully market the Paralympic Games and Paralympic athletes. These issues will be discussed and explored further in Chapter 6.

Chapter 7 explores some of the key issues with the modern day Paralympic Movement. From its inception in the late 1940s the founder of the international Paralympic Movement, Ludwig Guttmann, described the aims of his use of sport in the rehabilitation process of the spinally injured to be social re-integration and to change the perceptions of the non-disabled within society regarding what people with disabilities are capable of. This continued to be the underlying message of the International Paralympic Committee regarding the Paralympic Games and international disability sport for many years. These kind of aims and the language associated with it (e.g. social integration, changing perceptions, etc.) possibly lead to the Paralympic Games being perceived primarily as a cultural games rather than one that is about sport. Cultural games have as their aim an ethos of fostering self-respect and belief amongst their participants as well as helping to solidify their social identity as a group. Other examples of cultural games include the Gay Games and the Maccabiah Jewish Games. However, the last five years or so, have seen a distinct shift in the language used and the aims set out by the International Paralympic Committee towards a purely sport based outlook. Some of the reasons and implications of this move will be discussed.

Given the varying nature and impact of physical impairments and the number of different impairment groupings that participate in the Paralympic Games a system of classification has been developed over time to try and ensure fair and equitable competition. However, this often causes confusion for spectators unfamiliar with disability sport and has been accused of devaluing disability sport due to the increased number of medals this can lead to. The reasons for this will be explored and explained.

Much has been written about the illegal use of drugs for performance enhancement purposes within non-disabled sport. Drugs cheats also occur in disability sport. However, the problem is made far more difficult in disability sport by the fact that some athletes actually need to take drugs on a regular basis for health reasons. How this is handled within disability sport will be discussed and explained.

Chapter 7 will end with a discussion of a relatively new phenomenon that has nonetheless received a great deal of media attention over the last eighteen months. With the massive improvements in performance standards currently occurring in disability sport some athletes, notably Oscar Pistorius of South Africa, have reached a standard that might allow them to qualify for the Olympic Games. However, the technology they use in terms of adapted equipment in order to enable them to compete has raised questions regarding advantages such equipment might give them over their non-disabled counterparts. This has lead to the coining of such terms as 'technological doping' or 'cyborg athlete'.

Women and athletes with high support needs are the topic of Chapter 8. Some of the issues that arise out of the debate around the cultural versus sports model debate and the impacts they have had upon the participation rates for both women and athletes with high support needs are described and explored further.

Given the international nature of the Paralympic Games, Chapter 9 attempts to highlight the impacts of many of the issues raised in this book on a variety of nations. It does this through a series of 'snapshots' that describe how these issues may have impacted upon the participation and success of a particular nation at the Paralympic Games. These issues may be geographical, topographical, economic, political or cultural and may be specific to a particular country or may be relevant to other countries regionally or globally.

The final chapter will look at an issue that has long been a cause of confusion for many people with little or no knowledge of disability sport. Many of these individuals believe that the Special Olympics and the Paralympic Games are one and the same event. This chapter will explain the difference between the two. It will then go on to discuss the participation of athletes with an intellectual disability in the Paralympic Games and why they are currently banned from participation following the scandal that occurred with the Spanish Intellectually Disabled Basketball team at the Sydney 2000 Paralympic Games and the huge ramifications this had for the Paralympic Movement as a whole.

The approach of *The Paralympic Games Explained*

Disability sport in general and the Paralympic Games in particular, have grown hugely both in terms of size and political and media attention over the last twenty years. Despite this there is still a dearth of academic research or teaching regarding the subject. The aim of *The Paralympic Games Explained* is, therefore, first and foremost to provide an introductory resource that outlines the history, development and issues for the Paralympic Movement. *The Paralympic Games Explained* attempts to highlight the complex interactions that occur between disability, sport, the body and non-disabled society, how these interactions impact upon potential Paralympic athletes and how the Paralympic Movement and its constituent members attempt to deal with or mediate these impacts.

Each chapter contains study activities and chapter review questions in order to try and make the reader think more deeply about the issues raised. A large amount of factual information in the form of tables and graphs have been included, in addition to comparative information from the Olympic Movement where appropriate, in the hope that this might act as the starting point for further research of specific topics by the reader.

The ten chapters that make up *The Paralympic Games Explained* can all be studied in isolation, providing an introductory resource for each of the topics covered. However, given the complexity of many of the issues raised, and in order to facilitate a better overall understanding, there are a number of cross-references between the chapters.

1 The history and development of the Paralympic Games

Chapter aims

- Outline the history and development of the Summer and Winter Paralympic Games.
- Explain the development and various meanings of the term 'paralympic'.
- Outline the various impairment groupings that make up the Paralympic Movement.

Before proceeding with this chapter it is important to point out that the academic study of the history of the Paralympic Games is still in its infancy, especially compared to the historical study of events such as the Olympic Games. It is only in the last five to ten years that any serious attempts have been made to document their history and development. Also, unlike the Olympic Games, there is still no single archival or library source that adequately documents the subject. This problem has been further compounded by the fact that record keeping for these Games, especially prior to 1988, was quite basic, with much material connected to these early Games either simply lost, thrown out or in the case of the very first Paralympic Games in Rome in 1960, destroyed in a fire. Many of the reasons for this lack of record keeping will become clear throughout the text, but the main reasons appear to be that no one involved in these early Games believed that the Paralympic Games would ever reach a size or importance that would make them worthy of academic historical documentation and study and that the Games were organised on shoe-string budgets by volunteers who had little or no time to ensure the Games were adequately documented. The area in which this has had the greatest impact has been in arriving at accurate figures for athlete participation numbers at the early Games. Even where 'full' results are available, often in the case of team events and relays, only the country name is given rather than the names of the individual team members, making it impossible to come up with accurate figures for participating athletes either by country or gender. There is, however, now general agreement regarding the number of participating nations at each Games and the facts and figures that appear in this chapter are the result of over five years of research in this area by the author.

Disability sport prior to the 1940s

Sainsbury (1998) cites several examples of sports and leisure clubs for the disabled in the early part of the twentieth century, including the British Society of One-Armed Golfers (1932) and the 'Disabled Drivers' Motor Club (1922). Indeed the first international organisation responsible for a particular impairment group and its involvement in sport – Comité International des Sports des Sourds (CISS) – was set up by a deaf Frenchman, E. Rubens-Alcais, in 1924 with the support of six national sports federations for the deaf. In August 1924 the first International Silent Games was held in Paris with athletes from nine countries in attendance (DePauw and Gavron, 1995). Now called the Deaflympics there are Summer and Winter versions which occur in the year following their Olympic and Paralympic counterparts.

The impact of World War II on disability sport

Prior to World War II, the vast majority of those with spinal cord injuries died within three years following their injury (Legg *et al.*, 2002). Indeed, Ludwig Guttman, the universally accepted founder of the modern day Paralympic movement, whilst a doctor in 1930s Germany encountered on a ward round a coal miner with a broken back. Guttmann was shocked to learn from the consultant that such cases were a waste of time as he would be dead within two weeks (Craven, 2006). This was usually from sepsis of the blood or kidney failure or both. However, after World War II sulfa drugs made spinal cord injury survivable (Brandmeyer and McBee, 1986). The other major issue for individuals with spinal injuries was the major depression caused by societal attitudes to them, which, at the time, automatically assigned them to the scrapheap of life as useless and worthless individuals.

Ludwig Guttman was a German-Jewish neurologist who fled Nazi Germany with his family in 1939 and eventually settled in Oxford where he found work at Oxford University. In September 1943 the British Government commissioned Guttmann as the Director of the National Spinal Injuries Unit at the Ministry of Pensions Hospital, Stoke Mandeville, Aylesbury (Lomi *et al.*, 2004). This was mainly to take care of the numerous soldiers and civilians suffering from spinal injuries as a result of the war. Guttmann accepted under the condition that he would be totally independent and that he could apply his philosophy as far as the whole approach to the treatment of those patients was concerned, although many of his colleagues were apparently surprised by his enthusiasm for what they perceived as an utterly daunting task. Apparently, they could not understand how Guttmann could leave Oxford University to be 'engulfed in the hopeless and depressing task of looking after traumatic spinal paraplegics' (Goodman, 1986).

Prior to World War II there is little evidence of organised efforts to develop or promote sport for individuals with disabling conditions, especially those with spinal injuries who were considered to have no hope of surviving their injuries. Following the war, however, medical authorities were prompted to re-evaluate traditional methods of rehabilitation which were not satisfactorily responding to the medical and psychological needs of the large number of soldiers disabled in combat (Steadward, 1992). According to McCann (1996), Guttmann recognised the physiological and psychological values of sport in the rehabilitation of paraplegic hospital inpatients and so it was that sport was introduced as part of the total rehabilitation programme for patients in the spinal unit. The aim was not only to give hope and a sense of self-worth to the patients, but to change the attitudes of society towards the spinally injured by demonstrating to them that they could not only continue to be useful members of society, but could take part in activities and complete tasks most of the non-disabled society would struggle with (Anderson, 2003).

According to Guttmann (1952) they started modestly and cautiously with darts, snooker, punch-ball and skittles. Sometime later, apparently after Dr Guttman and his remedial gymnast, Quartermaster 'Q' Hill had 'waged furious battle' in an empty ward to test it, the sport of wheelchair polo was introduced. This was perceived a short time later, however, as too rough for all concerned and was replaced by wheelchair netball (Scruton, 1964). This later became what we now know as wheelchair basketball. The next sport to be introduced into the programme at Stoke Mandeville was to play a key role in all areas of Dr Guttman's rehabilitation plans. That sport was archery. According to Guttmann archery was of immense value in strengthening, in a very natural way, just those muscles of the upper limbs, shoulders and trunk, on which the paraplegic's well-balanced, upright position depends (Guttmann, 1952). However, it was far more than just that. It was one of the very few sports that, once proficient, paraplegics could compete on equal terms with their non-disabled counterparts. This led to visits of teams from Stoke Mandeville to a number of non-disabled archery clubs in later years, which were very helpful in breaking down the barriers between the public and the paraplegics. It also meant that once discharged from hospital the paraplegic had an access to society through their local archery club (Guttmann, 1952). According to Guttmann these experiments were the beginning of a systematic development of competitive sport for the paralysed as an essential part of their medical rehabilitation and social re-integration in the community of a country like Great Britain where sport in one form or another plays such an essential part in the life of so many people (Guttmann, 1976).

An inauspicious beginning to a worldwide phenomenon

For an event that would later go on to become the largest ever sporting event for people with disabilities and the second largest sporting event on the planet after the Olympic Games, the event now known globally as the Paralympic Games had a rather inauspicious beginning. It began life as an archery demonstration between two teams of paraplegics from the Ministry of Pensions Hospital at Stoke Mandeville and the Star and Garter Home for Injured War Veterans at Richmond in Surrey. It was held in conjunction with the presentation of a specially adapted bus to the patients of Stoke Mandeville by the British Legion and London Transport. Perhaps more auspicious was the date chosen for the handover of the bus and the archery demonstration, Thursday, 29 July 1948, the exact same day as the opening ceremony for the Games of the Fourteenth Olympiad at Wembley in London less than thirty-five miles away. It is difficult to assess whether this initial link to the Olympic Games was a deliberate one, or just coincidence, but it was a link that Guttmann himself would cultivate very overtly over the following years and decades. Guttmann later stated that the event was an experiment as a public performance, but also a demonstration to society that sport was not just the domain of the non-disabled (Guttmann, 1952). The aim of the bus was not only to allow patients to travel around the country to various activities and events, but also to allow them to get back out into the community and enter more into the life of the town. The bus would also be used to take competitors to many more archery competitions over the coming years against teams of both disabled and non-disabled archers.

Dr Guttmann's 'Grand Festival of Paraplegic Sport', as the second incarnation of the Games were described, were held on Wednesday, 27 July 1949. Building upon much hard work done by Dr Guttmann, his staff and the impact of various Stoke Mandeville patients moving to other spinal units around the country and taking their new found enthusiasm for sport with them the number of spinal units entered rose to six (The Cord, 1949). A grand total of thirty-seven individuals took part in these Games and with the exception of the archers from the Polish Hospital at Penley every competitor had, at some time, been a patient of Dr Guttmann. In addition to a repeat of the previous year's archery competition, 'net-ball' was added to the programme for these Games. This was a kind of hybrid of netball and basketball played in wheelchairs and using netball posts for goals.

The next three years saw competitor numbers at the Games continue to grow as more and more spinal units from around the country began to enter teams. Guttmann, however, had far grander plans and continued with the hope that he could move the Games on to an international footing. One local paper claimed this had moved a step closer in 1951 with representation of competitors with a variety of nationalities including a Frenchman, an Australian, some Poles and a Southern Rhodesian. With the exception of the Poles, who were residents of the Polish hospital at Penley, the others were all individual patients resident at British Spinal Units. The first step to Guttmann's dream was to occur the very next year, 1952, when a team of four paraplegics from the Military Rehabilitation Centre, Aardenburg, near Doorn in the Netherlands became the first truly international competitors at the Games. Over the next four years the international nature of the Games rose dramatically so that in 1956 there were eighteen nations represented at

Table 1.1 A chronology of the early Stoke Mandeville Games (1948–1959)

Date	Teams	Competitors	Sports	New sport
Thurs 29 July 1948	2*	16	1	Archery
Weds 29 July 1949	6*	37	2	'Netball'
Weds 27 July 1950	10*	61	3	Javelin
Sat 28 July 1951	11*	126	4	Snooker
Sat 26 July, 1952	2	130	5	Table tennis
Sat 8 August 1953	6	200	6	Swimming
Sat 31 July 1954	14	250	7	Dartchery
Fri and Sat 29–30 July 1955	18	280	8	Fencing. Basketball replaced netball
Fri and Sat 27–28 July 1956	18	300	8	–
Fri and Sat 26–27 July 1957	24	360	9	Shot Putt
Thurs–Sat 24–26 July 1958	21	350	10	Throwing the club
Thurs–Sat 23–25 July 1959	20	360	11	Pentathlon

* Number of Spinal Units participating

the Games and a total of twenty-one different nations had competed since 1952 (Scruton, 1956).

Spreading the word

It might appear hard to understand how an event that started life with just sixteen wheelchair archers in 1948 as a demonstration to the public that competitive sport is not the prerogative of the non-disabled could, just ten years later, find itself with several dozen international teams in attendance. In fact the Games grew to such an extent that despite several extensions to the accommodation it became necessary to introduce a national Stoke Mandeville Games from 1958 onwards from which a British team would be selected to take part in the international Games a month or so later (Scruton, 1957). There appear to be five possible mechanisms that played key roles in spreading the word regarding the Stoke Mandeville Games to various corners of the globe:

1   In the early years much of the driving force for the growth appears to have been down to former patients of Dr Guttmann's who were transferred to other spinal units and took what they had learnt, and their enthusiasm for it, with them. Many of them returned year after year to take part in the Games. To a slightly lesser extent this is also true of the doctors and surgeons from all over the world who visited Stoke Mandeville to train under Dr Guttmann and then returned home and incorporated sport into their treatment programmes, such as Dr Ralph Spira from Israel.

2   In 1947 the very first edition of *The Cord* was published. This contained articles and advice of benefit to paraplegics everywhere and often gave

space to reports on the sporting events at the hospital. Because practical information of assistance to paraplegics was in short supply copies of this journal often got sent abroad to individuals and organisations carrying news of the Games and Dr Guttmann's rehabilitation methods far and wide. The journal continued to be published up to 1983.

3   Dr Guttmann himself was a major player in spreading the word about the Games. He would often travel abroad to conferences, to give lectures and even to give evidence in court cases and would take every opportunity to tell people about the Games and his use of sport as a rehabilitative tool. He would often challenge particular key individuals in other countries to bring a team to the Games the following year as was the case with Sir George Bedbrooke at the Royal Perth Hospital on a visit in 1956. Australia sent their first team to Stoke Mandeville the following year (Lockwood and Lockwood, 2007).

4   Dr Guttmann also appears to have been very astute when it comes to politics and what it takes to get an event noticed. Right from the very first Games in 1948 he made sure that high ranking political and social figures and later sports stars and celebrities were present at the Games in order to attract profile and media attention.

5   The final mechanism used by Dr Guttmann to cement the importance of the Games in people's minds, despite the lukewarm response it received when he first suggested it, was his constant comparisons to the Olympic Games. It's affect and design appears to have been two-fold. First, to give his patients something tangible to aim for and to give them a feeling of self-worth and, second, to catch the attention of the media and people and organisations involved with paraplegics worldwide.

The birth of the Paralympic Games

Guttmann's persistence in forging a link between the Stoke Mandeville Games and the Olympic Games, which will be outlined in greater detail in Chapter 2, took a giant leap forward at the annual meeting of the World Veterans Federation in Rome in May, 1959. Following discussions with various individuals from the Instituto Nazionale per l'Assicurazione contro gli Infortuni sul Lavoro (INAIL) and Dr Maglio of the Spinal Unit, Ostia, Rome, it was agreed to host the 1960 Games in Rome a few weeks after the Olympic Games were to take place in the same city (The Cord, 1960). Despite a few problems in Rome, mainly around access to accommodation, the Games were considered a resounding success. Immediately the possibility of Tokyo, already chosen by the International Olympic Committee (IOC) to host the Olympics in 1964, also hosting the Stoke Mandeville Games was voiced. An invitation to the Japanese to host the Games in 1964 led to a team of eight officials and their first ever athletes attending the Stoke Mandeville Games in 1962 and, ultimately led to their acceptance to host the 1964 Games. Present at the Tokyo Games was Dr Leonardo Ruiz, from the Instituto Mexicano de Rehabilitación, as part of an observation team looking at the possibilities for the Games to be held in Mexico City, hosts for the Olympic Games of 1968. According to the minutes of the International Stoke Mandeville Games Committee dated 21 July 1965 a letter from the head of the rehabilitation centre stating that things were progressing well was read out. Due to the worries about the impact of the altitude on paraplegics it was decided that the Americans should take a team to Mexico City to investigate. However, when their team manager, Ben Lipton, tried to arrange this he received a letter from the President of the rehabilitation centre stating that due to financial constraints and accessibility issues with facilities Mexico City would be unable to host the Games. Following offers from both New York, and Tel Aviv it was decided that the 1968 Games would be held in Israel.

Following the Games in Israel, it was again hoped that the Games would return to being hosted by the Olympic host city in 1972, which was to be Munich. Unfortunately, the Olympic Organising Committee declined the application on the basis that the Olympic village was to be converted into housing immediately after the Games and it was, apparently, too late to change this. The Germans did, however, offer the alternative of the University of Heidelberg, which was accepted. The Olympic Games of 1976 were scheduled to take place in Montreal, Canada, but once again it was decided by the Montreal organisers to decline the invitation to host the Games, especially in view of the fact that it had been decided to hold a combined International Stoke Mandeville Games Federation (ISMGF)-International Sports Organisation for the Disabled (ISOD) Games consisting of paraplegics, blind and amputee athletes, which added to both the size and the complexity of the Games. The Games eventually took place in Toronto. In July 1977 the decision was taken to award the 1980 Paralympic Games to Arnhem in the Netherlands, following lack of response from the Olympic organisers in Moscow. The Olympic Games of 1984 were set to take place in Los Angeles. However, no evidence can be found that any attempt was made by ISMGF or ISOD to secure the use of the Los Angeles venues for their own games. Following a bid by Ben Lipton, Chairman of the US National Wheelchair Athletic Association (NWAA) in 1980, America was still selected to be the host country. These Games were, however to be split into ISMGF Games, to be organised by the NWAA and ISOD Games to be organised by ISOD at a separate venue at around the same time. According to the final report of the VIIth World Wheelchair Games (1984) in October 1980 Ben Lipton had issued a position paper stating the reasons for NWAA's decision to hold separate games. With the decision finally taken for this plan to go ahead, the wheelchair Games were set to take place at the University of Illinois, Urbana-Champaign in July, with the ISOD 'International Games for the Disabled' taking place in Nassau County, New York in June. However, political and fundraising problems around the wheelchair Games forced the University of Illinois to withdraw their support for the Games in early

1984 and the wheelchair Games were transferred at very short notice to Stoke Mandeville. From 1988 onwards the Summer Paralympic Games have been held in the same host city as the Olympic Games beginning about two weeks after the Olympic Closing Ceremony. The only exception to this was the Paralympic Games for Intellectually Disabled Athletes that was held in Madrid in 1992 as a precursor to Intellectually Disabled athletes being added to the programme alongside the other four impairment groups in Atlanta four years later.

The Winter Paralympic Games

The idea for a Winter Paralympic Games was first suggested at the annual general meeting of the International Sports Organisation for the Disabled in 1974. Perhaps, unsurprisingly, the idea came from the Swedish delegation, a country with a strong winter sports tradition. With less than eighteen months in which to make the necessary arrangements the resulting Games were quite small in size, but hailed as a great success nonetheless. These first Games only catered for athletes with amputations or visual impairments. The first six incarnations of the Games all took place in Europe, where winter sports were highly developed and winter sports for athletes with disabilities first began in the 1950s. Athletes with spinal injuries joined the second Games in Geilo, Norway and they were quickly joined by cerebral palsied and Les Autres athletes in Innsbruck, Austria four years later. The Winter Games did not occur at the Olympic host city venues until their fifth incarnation in Tignes-Albertville in 1992, although demonstration events for disability skiing were held at the Sarajevo Winter Olympic Games as early as 1984.

Study Activity

Study Table 1.2. Make a list of possible reasons why participation in the Paralympic Games varies so much by continent. Remember these reasons may be different for the Summer and Winter Games and may also be different for some countries in the same continent.

Development of sport for other impairments groups

Before continuing it is important here to give a brief history of the development of sport for the other main impairment groups e.g. the blind, amputees, etc. In 1960, recognising the need to organise international sports for disability groups other than paraplegics the International Working Group on Sports for the Disabled was set up under the aegis of the World Veterans Federation whose headquarters was in Paris. Unfortunately, due to language difficulties and differences of opinion the organisation failed

Table 1.2 A chronology of the Summer and Winter Paralympic Games

Year	Location	No. of countries	Europe	Americas	Africa	Asia	Oceania	No. of athletes	Impairment groups included
1960	Rome, Italy	21	16	2	1	1	1	~ 400	SCI
1964	Tokyo, Japan	21	12	2	2	3	2	375	SCI
1968	Tel Aviv, Israel	28	16	4	3	3	2	~ 800	SCI
1972	Heidelberg, West Germany	42	23	7	5	5	2	~ 1000	SCI
1976	**Örnsköldsvik, Sweden**	**16**	**12**	**2**	**2**	**1**	**0**	**198**	**A, BVI**
1976	Toronto, Canada	40	19	10	3	5	3	~ 1650	SCI, A, BVI
1980	**Geilo, Norway**	**18**	**12**	**2**	**1**	**1**	**2**	**299**	**SCI, A, BVI**
1980	Arnhem, The Netherlands	42	22	8	5	5	2	~ 1900	SCI, A, BVI, CP
1984	**Innsbruck, Austria**	**21**	**16**	**2**	**0**	**1**	**2**	**419**	**SCI, ALA, BVI, CP**
1984	Stoke Mandeville, UK &	41	19	10	3	6	3	~ 1100	SCI
	New York, USA	45	25	6	3	9	2	~ 1700	ALA, BVI, CP
1988	**Innsbruck, Austria**	**22**	**17**	**2**	**0**	**1**	**2**	**377**	**SCI, ALA, BVI, CP**
1988	Seoul, South Korea	60	27	11	4	16	2	3058	SCI, ALA, BVI, CP
1992	**Tignes-Albertville, France**	**24**	**18**	**2**	**0**	**2**	**2**	**365**	**SCI, ALA, BVI, CP**
1992	Barcelona, Spain &	83*	33	16	11	20	2	3001	SCI, ALA, BVI, CP
	Madrid, Spain	75	28	22	13	11	1	~1400	ID
1994	**Lillehammer, Norway**	**31**	**24**	**2**	**0**	**3**	**2**	**471**	**SCI, ALA, BVI, CP**
1996	Atlanta, USA	103	41	18	16	25	3	3261	SCI, ALA, BVI, CP, ID
1998	**Nagano, Japan**	**31**	**22**	**2**	**1**	**4**	**2**	**561**	**SCI, ALA, BVI, CP, ID**
2000	Sydney, Australia	122*	41	20	20	33	7	3882	SCI, ALA, BVI, CP, ID
2002	**Salt Lake, USA**	**36**	**25**	**3**	**1**	**5**	**2**	**416**	**SCI, ALA, BVI, CP**
2004	Athens, Greece	135	42	24	28	36	5	3808	SCI, ALA, BVI, CP
2006	**Torino, Italy**	**38**	**25**	**4**	**1**	**6**	**2**	**474**	**SCI, ALA, BVI, CP**
2008	Beijing, P.R. China	146	45	24	30	40	7	3951	SCI, ALA, BVI, CP

* Includes a group entitled independent Paralympic athletes. Bold = Winter Paralympic Games. SCI = Spinal cord injury, A = Amputee, BVI = Blind and visually impaired, CP = Cerebral palsied, ALA = Amputee and les autres, ID = Intellectually disabled

and was dissolved in 1964 (Guttmann, 1976). In its place the International Sports Organisation for the Disabled (ISOD) was founded at a meeting in Paris in 1964 (Scruton, 1998). ISOD remained under the patronage of the World Veterans Federation until 1967, when it became an independent organisation and its headquarters were transferred to Stoke Mandeville. In the same year the British Limbless Ex-Servicemen's Association (BLESMA) organised the first ever international sports competition for amputees at Stoke Mandeville. Guttmann, now Sir Ludwig Guttmann after being knighted by the Queen for services to the disabled in 1966, became President of both ISMGF and ISOD and this dual role would play a major part in bringing the disability groups together in one Games. Initially ISOD represented a number of disability groups, but by 1981 both the blind and the cerebral palsied had broken away to form their own international federations. In 2004 ISOD, then representing Amputees and Les Autres merged with the International Stoke Mandeville Wheelchair Sports Federation (ISMWSF) to form the International Wheelchair and Amputee Sports Federation (IWAS). As stated above, initially ISOD represented a number of disability groups and together with ISMGF co-operated in the organisation of the Summer Paralympic Games in Toronto, 1976 and Arnhem, 1980. They also initiated the first ever Winter Paralympic Games in Örnsköldsvik, Sweden in 1976 which was just for amputee athletes and those who were blind or visually impaired.

The term 'paralympic'

There is often confusion as to where the the term 'paralympic' derives from. Girginov and Parry (2005) claim that it is a misconception that the word 'paralympic' derives from the term paraplegic. In its current modern-day usage this is true, but historically this claim is inaccurate. The earliest written use of the term appears in the summer issue of *The Cord* in 1951, when David Hinds, a Paraplegic at Stoke Mandeville hospital wrote an article entitled 'Alice at the Paralympiad', which was a skit on Alice in Wonderland. However, what this article does not explain is how the term came about. A possible clue comes from two articles in a special edition of *The Cord* celebrating ten years of the Spinal Unit in 1954. In one article Dora T. Bell, the physiotherapist attached to the unit, refers to the 'Paraolympics of Stoke Mandeville' and in a second article Ward Sister Merchant refers to the 'Paraplegic Olympics'. It would appear then that this early usage of the term is an amalgamation of the words paraplegic and Olympics, which was shortened further to 'Paralympics', possibly because it is smoother and shorter to pronounce. What is also clear from the increasing usage of the term 'paralympic' by the media during the 1950s is that it was used to refer to all the Games held annually from 1948–1959 as is reinforced by the heading in the *New York Times* of 21 August, 1960 which stated 'US to send 24 Athletes to Rome for Annual 'Paralympics' Event'.

The deliberate linking of the Stoke Mandeville Games with the host city of the Olympic Games every fourth year had an almost immediate impact on press usage of the term Paralympics. A good example of this is the local newspaper, the *Bucks Advertiser and Aylesbury News*, the first paper to use the term Paralympic back in 1953. In reporting on the Games at Stoke Mandeville from 1961 to 1963 it reverted to describing them as the International Stoke Mandeville Games. It appears that once the much clearer link between the Stoke Mandeville Games and the Olympic Games had been made by moving them away from Stoke Mandeville to the same city chosen to host the Olympic Games the usage of the term 'paralympic', still in its 'Paraplegic Olympics' context, became much more specific. It now only referred to the edition of the International Stoke Mandeville Games held in the Olympic year.

The modern day usage of the term 'paralympic' came about as a result of the participation in the Games of impairment groups other than those with spinal cord injuries in Toronto in 1976. As they now included blind and visually impaired and amputee athletes they could no longer be called the International Stoke Mandeville Games, nor could the term 'paralympic' as it was then understood (Paraplegic Olympics) be applied. The next few versions of the Games used varying adaptations of the term Olympics for the Disabled, which led to quite heated discussions with the International Olympic Committee over the use of Olympic terminology. In the end the IOC agreed to the use of the term 'paralympic' being used for the Games from 1988 onwards, where at the same time the Games finally returned to being hosted by the same city as the Olympic Games. A pattern that has occurred ever since. However, the use of the term 'paralympic' derives from the Greek preposition 'para' meaning 'next to' giving a meaning of parallel or next to the Olympic Games.

Impairment groups at the Paralympic Games

The participants at the current Summer and Winter Paralympic Games are drawn from four impairment groups:

Athletes with spinal cord injuries

Athletes with spinal cord injuries includes all those athletes suffering from a spinal cord lesion, spina bifida or polio. Athletes with spinal cord Injuries can also be split into two broad categories of paraplegics which involves a 'neurologic affliction of both legs' and quadriplegics or tetraplegics which involves a 'neurologic affliction of all four extremities' (Auxter *et al.*, 1993).

Cerebral palsied athlete

Cerebral palsy is a condition in which damage inflicted on the brain has led to motor function disorder (Auxter *et al.*, 1993). According to French (1997) there are three types of cerebral palsy. There is spastic that is characterised by tense muscles which are contracted and resistant to movement, *arthetoid* that is characterised by involuntary movements of the affected body parts and *ataxia* that is characterised by a disturbance or lack of balance and coordination.

Amputees and les autres athletes

The classification system for athletes with amputations includes only those athletes with acquired or congenital amputations. Les autres, literally meaning 'the others' includes all motor disabilities except amputees, medullar lesions and cerebral palsy, for example muscular dystrophy, multiple sclerosis, arthrogryposis, Friedrich's ataxia and arthritis (Bazylewicz, 1998). This grouping also includes athletes with dwarfism.

Blind and visually impaired athletes

This group of athletes ranges from individuals who are totally blind to individuals who can recognise objects or contours between 2 and 6 metres away that a person with normal vision can see at 60 metres (i.e. 2/60 to 6/60 vision) and/or a field of vision between 5 and 20 degrees.

There is one other group of athletes whose international representative organisation is a member of the International Paralympic Committee. These are athletes with an intellectual disability. Although athletes with an intellectual disability have previously competed at the Paralympic Games they are currently banned from participation. For an explanation of the situation regarding intellectually disabled athletes in the Paralympic Games please see Chapter 10.

Upcoming Paralympic Games

The Vancouver 2010 Winter Paralympic Games

The opening ceremony for the Vancouver 2010 Winter Paralympic Games will take place on the 12 March, with the closing ceremony scheduled for 21 March. It is expected that a maximum of 600 athletes from an expected forty-five nations will participate in sixty-four events spread across the following sports: alpine skiing, ice sledge hockey, Nordic skiing (biathlon and cross country), wheelchair curling.

Currently athletes from four impairment groups are scheduled to compete in Vancouver. These are amputee and les autres athletes, blind and visually impaired athletes, cerebral palsied athletes and athletes with spinal cord injuries.

Further details on the Vancouver 2010 Winter Paralympic Games can be found at www.Vancouver2010.com.

The London 2012 Summer Paralympic Games

The opening ceremony for the London 2012 Summer Paralympic Games will take place on the 29 August, with the closing ceremony scheduled for 9 September. It is expected that a maximum of 4,200 athletes from an expected 150 nations will participate in 480 events spread across the following sports: athletics, archery, Boccia, cycling, equestrianism, football (five-a-side), football (seven-a-side), goalball, judo, powerlifting, rowing, sailing, shooting, swimming, table tennis, volleyball, wheelchair basketball, wheelchair fencing, wheelchair rugby, wheelchair tennis.

Currently athletes from four impairment groups are scheduled to compete in London. These are amputee and les autres athletes, blind and visually impaired athletes, cerebral palsied athletes and athletes with spinal cord injuries. Discussions about the participation of Intellectually Disabled athletes in London are currently ongoing. Further details on the London 2012 Summer Paralympic Games can be found at www.London2012.com.

The Sochi 2014 Winter Paralympic Games

The opening ceremony for the Sochi 2014 Winter Paralympic Games will take place on the Friday 7 March, with the closing ceremony scheduled for Sunday 16 March. Athletes will participate in the following sports: Alpine skiing, ice sledge hockey, Nordic skiing (biathlon and cross country), wheelchair curling.

Currently athletes from four impairment groups are scheduled to compete in Sochi. These are amputee and les autres athletes, blind and visually impaired athletes, cerebral palsied athletes and athletes with spinal cord injuries. Further information on the Sochi 2014 Winter Paralympic Games can be accessed at www.Sochi2014.com.

2016 Host City?

A decision on the host city for the 2016 Olympic and Paralympic Games will be made at the IOC Session in Copenhagen on 2 October 2009. The shortlisted candidates following visits by the IOC Evaluation Commission, which included a member of the IPC Governing Board, are Chicago, Madrid, Rio de Janiero, and Tokyo.

Conclusion

International disability sport has come an amazingly long way since its early beginnings as a rehabilitative tool at a hospital in England over sixty years ago. It has developed into a huge international mega-event that has done a great deal to raise the awareness of what people with disabilities are capable of and is increasingly making disability sport and athletes with disabilities an important and visible part of the international sporting calendar.

Chapter review questions

1   What factors led Dr Guttmann to introduce sport as part of the rehabilitation process and what were his aims in doing so?
2   What were the key mechanisms by which interest in the Stoke Mandeville Games spread?
3   Explain the different uses of the term 'paralympic' and how each came about.
4   Name the six different impairment groupings that have participated in the Paralympic Games.

Suggested further reading

International Paralympic Committee, 2006, *Paralympic Winter Games 1976–2006: Örnsköldsvik*, Turin, RLC, Paris, France.
Scruton, J., 1998, *Stoke Mandeville: Road to the Paralympics*, Peterhouse Press, Aylesbury, UK.

2 The Olympic Movement and the Paralympic Games

Chapter aims

- Outline the development of the relationship between the modern Olympic Movement and the Paralympic Games.
- Outline the impacts of the recent close working relationship between the two organisations.

As stated in Chapter 1, the very first Stoke Mandeville Games coincided with the Opening Ceremony for the Fourteenth Olympic Games in London, which Guttmann later claimed to be mere coincidence. However, at the end of the second Stoke Mandeville Games the very next year Dr Guttmann gave a speech in which he made the claim that the Stoke Mandeville Games would one day become recognised as the paraplegic's equivalent of the Olympic Games. This certainly showed remarkable foresight given that he himself admits that, despite the widely accepted success of the day, the statement was met with very little shared optimism from those gathered in the audience (Guttmann, 1954). It did, however, prompt one of the local papers, the *Bucks Advertiser and Aylesbury News* dated 29 July, to print an article under the headline '"Olympic Games" of Disabled Men is Born at Stoke'. When the Stoke Mandeville Games first became truly international in 1952 with the participation of a Dutch team, Guttmann used this opportunity to reinforce the Olympic link further when, during his opening speech, he apparently reminded those present that the Olympic Games were in progress in Helsinki and that he hoped that the paraplegic Games, as the author called them, would become as international and widely known as the Olympic Games (Guttmann, 1952).

Four years later at the Games of 1956 some of the prizes were presented by Sir (later Lord) Arthur Porritt, himself a surgeon and also an IOC member for Great Britain. Apparently the Games so impressed him that a few weeks later he wrote to Otto Mayer, Chancellor of the IOC, nominating the Games for the Fearnley Cup. The nomination went forward and at their session held in conjunction with the Olympic Games in Melbourne two months later the members voted to award the Fearnley Cup to the Stoke Mandeville

Games. This was the first time the cup had ever been awarded to a British organisation or any kind of disability sport organisation anywhere. The award of the Fearnley Cup motivated Dr Guttmann to dream of far bigger things, as is shown in the report of his opening speech at the 1957 Games when, with reference to the Fearnley Cup he is reported in the *Bucks Herald* dated 2 August to have stated that he hoped this would be only the beginning of a closer connection between the Stoke Mandeville Games and the Olympic Games. He apparently went on to say that after the splendid recognition by the Olympic Committee in awarding them the Fearnley Cup he hoped that the Olympic Games would soon be open to disabled sportsmen and women. Another local newspaper, the *Bucks Advertiser and Aylesbury News*, also dated 2 August, reported him speaking about his greatest dream – that paraplegics might take part in the next Olympic Games, in Rome, having their own section.

Although Guttmann didn't exactly get his wish, the Games of 1960 did take place in Rome and these Games are now officially recognised as the first 'Paralympic Games'. However, despite Guttmann's clear efforts to forge a link with the Olympic Games he still insisted that the Games were called, and advertised as, the International Stoke Mandeville Games. Labanowich (1989) puts this reluctance down to a desire to retain the identity of the Games with Stoke Mandeville. The minutes of the International Stoke Mandeville Games Committee, dated 21 July 1965, whilst clearly supporting this theory, also note that the International Olympic Committee had 'raised the strongest objections to the use of the word "Paralympics"', although no other proof has been found to support this. Scruton (1998), however, puts forward a different theory from Labanowich. She claims that Guttmann regarded the athletes as having truly Olympic stature and that the Games were worthy of the title 'Olympics of the Paralysed', a version of which would come to greater prominence in 1976 and would eventually lead to great changes in the world of international disability sport.

The use of Olympic terminology (1973–1984)

Over the next decade very little evidence can be found of any dialogue or communication between the IOC and the international disability sport movement. However, the bringing together of athletes from both ISMGF and ISOD into one Games in Toronto in 1976 raised two problems with regards to a name for the Games. As they now included blind and amputee athletes they could no longer be called the International Stoke Mandeville Games, nor could the term 'Paralympic', as it was then understood (Paraplegic Olympics), be applied. In the end, the committees of ISMGF and ISOD decided to call the games in Toronto the Olympiad for the Physically Disabled, which the organisers shortened to the 'Torontolympiad', and ISOD, who were organising the first winter Games in Sweden, chose to call these games the Winter Olympics for the Disabled. The subject of the choice of names, according to papers held in the IOC archives was first drawn to the attention of the IOC by a letter from the International Ski Federation in September 1975. In it the Secretary General, Sigge Bergman, states that Bengt Hollen, Head of the organising committee for the disabled winter games claims that Sir Ludwig had been given the right, verbally, to use the term 'Olympic Games' for Stoke Mandeville competitions. In response Madame Berlioux wrote to Guttmann regarding the Ski Federation's letter and made it clear that no authority had been given either verbally or in writing allowing the use of the terms Olympic or Olympiad and asking both ISMGF and ISOD to refrain from doing so. Six days later IOC President, Lord Killanin, sent Madame Berlioux a memo stating that a meeting should be arranged with Guttmann and that in the interests of both the Olympic Movement and humanity it would be advisable for the IOC to encourage such activities provided the situation was absolutely clear.

In the meantime, Guttmann, obviously taken aback by the letter from the IOC, went on the offensive with a three page reply as to why the disability sports movement was entitled to use Olympic terminology and why it would not stop. These can be summed up in the following points:

1   Guttmann clearly considered the IOC to have recognised ISMGF as an 'Olympic Organisation' through the awarding of the Fearnley Cup in 1956.
2   He considered the disabled games to be the real Olympics because they adhered far more closely to the ideals of the founder Pierre de Coubertin.
3   The term 'Olympic' or 'Olympics' could be found in the London telephone directory applied to a wide variety of services including cleaners and hair salons.

Finally Guttmann makes it clear that until the IOC included Games for the disabled within the Olympic Games the disabled sports movement would continue to call their Games 'Olympics'.

Study activity

Analyse Guttman's claim that the disabled games were 'the real Olympics because they adhered far more closely to the ideals of the founder Pierre de Coubertin'. Could the same claim be made of the modern Paralympic Games?

Three weeks later Guttmann received a response from Madame Berlioux, claiming there had obviously been a misunderstanding with regard to the relationship between the IOC and ISMGF. She stated that the IOC were anxious to assist and give patronage to ISMGF and requested that a meeting be arranged with Lord Killanin. A meeting between Sir Ludwig and Lord Killanin took place over the Christmas period that year. The outcome of the meeting appears to have been that the IOC would provide assistance and patronage to the disability sports movement in return for an agreement that they would desist from using Olympic terminology after the Toronto Games. Killanin resolved to get agreement in principle for IOC recognition of ISMGF at the IOC session in Innsbruck following a careful scrutinisation of the ISMGF statutes. Lord Killanin again wrote to Sir Ludwig in March to confirm that following a debate by the IOC Executive Board a decision had been taken that the recognition of ISMGF was agreed 'in principle' provided they refrained from the use of Olympic terminology after Toronto. Final recognition was to be given following a final check to ensure that all ISMGF rules were 'fully in compliance with the Rules, Regulations and Principles of the IOC'. The Technical Director of the IOC wrote to Sir Ludwig in May with a series of questions, which Sir Ludwig quickly responded to.

With the exception of some correspondence in which Sir Ludwig sent Madame Berlioux and Lord Killanin a report of the Games in Toronto, communication between the IOC and Sir Ludwig went very quiet until early 1978. In the meantime, despite concerted efforts by Sir Ludwig, he failed to persuade the Russians to host the 1980 Games and so at a joint meeting of ISMGF and ISOD in July 1977 it was decided that Arnhem in the Netherlands should host them. It was also agreed that Geilo in Norway should host the winter games, which would this time be organised as a joint ISMGF-ISOD operation as paraplegics would be taking part for the first time. The summer games were to be entitled the Olympics for the Disabled 1980 and the winter games the second Winter Olympics for the Disabled. This came to the attention of the IOC and in February 1978 Madame Berlioux again wrote to Sir Ludwig regarding the use of Olympic terminology. Sir Ludwig responded by stating that he was still awaiting official written confirmation of the IOC decision to recognise ISMGF. Throughout the remainder of 1978 correspondence flowed backwards and forwards between Madame Berlioux and Sir Ludwig in order that a solution could be found and patronage officially bestowed upon ISMGF by the IOC. However, throughout this period several issues arose, both politically and practically, that prevented a solution being reached. These included the use of the term 'Olympic' by the Special Olympics organisation in the USA who had been granted use of the term by the United States Olympic Committee. This came to light when the Special Olympics Organisation made an application to join ISOD in 1978. In addition, the IOC wished to officially recognise only one organisation representing the whole of the disabled sports movement and despite ISOD and ISMGF having the same President in Sir Ludwig they were constitutionally two separate entities (see Chapter 3 for further details). Finally, South Africa was a full member of both ISOD and ISMGF and competed with a totally racially integrated team. However, the IOC stance at the time was that South Africa was banned from Olympic competition and they, therefore, felt unable to recognise an organisation that allowed South Africa to participate.

In the autumn of 1979, less than three months after his eightieth birthday, Sir Ludwig suffered a coronary thrombosis and despite a brief recovery died in March 1980 (Goodman, 1986). News of Sir Ludwig's death was obviously slow in reaching the IOC as in an internal memo in late March 1980 Lord Killanin wrote to Madame Berlioux that he thought they had not heard from Sir Ludwig for a while because he had become very old. He ends the memo by stating that nevertheless 'the correct thing would be that (a) these Games should not take place in the Olympic country (b) they should not be called the Olympic Games but whatever games they like, under the patronage of the IOC'. With the death of Sir Ludwig the attitude of the IOC seemed to harden somewhat as the possibility of litigation was raised for the first time. First, Madame Berlioux wrote to Mr Idenburg, President of the Netherlands Olympic Committee in May 1980 asking him if anything could be done under Dutch law to stop the use of the title 'Olympics for the Disabled'. Then, rather bizarrely, considering the Games finished on 5 July she wrote to Mr Henrik Meijers, Managing Director of the Sports Division for the Games on 17 October, asking if it was not too late for him to drop the word 'Olympics'. She concludes by indicating the possibility of litigation.

With the decision to host a split site Games in the USA in 1984 the way was now open to resurrect the use of the term 'Paralympic' and for the first time ever actually officially attach it to the ISMGF Games, which would be just for Paraplegics. The Games were set to take place at the University of Illinois, Urbana-Champaign in July. From the very beginning the organising committee called themselves the 1984 Paralympics Steering Committee and used as its logo the three intertwined circles, originally three wheelchair wheels, that had been used by ISMGF for several decades. The United States Olympic Committee (USOC) took exception to both the name and the three ringed logo claiming in a letter from their Executive Director, F. Don Miller to Dale Wiley, Chairman of the Steering Committee that they 'may tend to cause confusion with the Olympic Games'. USOC objections continued and in 1983 Dr Robert Jackson, the new President of ISMGF wrote to the new President of the IOC, Juan Antonio Samaranch asking for IOC approval of the name and logo. Samaranch responded by saying that the IOC saw no objection to the request, but that final responsibility lay with USOC.

Closer working relations with the IOC

This apparent thawing of attitudes within the IOC to the term 'Paralympic' came about following a number of meetings and events that assisted in a closer working relationship between the IOC and the disability sports movement and which are discussed in more detail in Chapter 3. A meeting took place between the International Co-ordinating Committee (ICC) (see Chapter 3) and the IOC in February 1983, at which IOC President Samaranch made it clear that the IOC wished the disabled sports movement to become part of the Olympic Movement. In return for the dropping of Olympic terminology from their events he was willing to offer the disabled sports movement, amongst other things, IOC patronage and financial assistance. One of the major results of this meeting was an agreement by the IOC that a demonstration disabled skiing event could take place at the Sarajevo Winter Olympic Games in 1984 and if successful a demonstration event might also be added to the Los Angeles Summer Games. This was confirmed at a meeting of the IOC Executive Board in early summer of 1983. Prior to all this in late 1982 the IOC had already shown a willingness to work closely with the disabled sports movement when at its Executive Board meeting in October 1982 it had agreed to give patronage to and allow the use of the Olympic rings in the logo for what were to be called the 1984 World Winter Games for the Disabled. This had been granted on the understanding that the term 'Olympic' would be dropped from ISOD's preferred title of 'Third Winter Olympic Games for the Disabled'. IOC President Samaranch also agreed to attend the Games in person.

The closer working relationship between ICC and the IOC paved the way for much closer links between the Olympic Movement and the disability sports movement, culminating in the 'Paralympic Games' returning in 1988 to the same city (Seoul, Korea), venues and village as the Olympic Games for the first time since 1964, a pattern that has been repeated at every summer and winter games since then. The impact of the Paralympic Games, especially the Summer Games, returning to the same host city and venues as the Olympic Games can clearly be seen in Figure 2.1 where the number of countries participating in the Paralympic Games has risen almost exponentially since 1988, with the number of nations participating having risen by 150 per cent between Seoul, 1988 and Beijing, 2008. Although participation at the Paralympic Winter Games by nations is far lower than for the Summer Paralympics there has still been a 58 per cent increase in the number of nations participating between Tignes-Albertville, 1992 and Turin, 2006.

Study activity

Study Figure 2.1. Try and account for the dramatic differences in the growth of the number of nations participating in the summer and Winter Paralympic Games.

Seoul, 1988 marked the return of the Paralympic Games to the same host city and venues for the first time in twenty-four years and a period of unprecedented change and growth within the movement. However the next few years also saw yet another period of tension between the IOC and the Paralympic Movement. The cause of this tension was the logo adopted by the Seoul Paralympic Organising Committee that the ICC and then the newly formed International Parlympic Committee (IPC), one year later, decided to adopt as the logo for the movement. The logo consisted of five

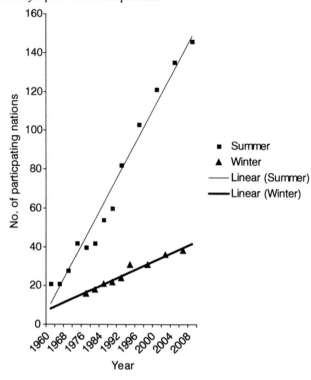

Figure 2.1 Growth in Participating Nations at the Summer and Winter Paralympic Games (with trend-line for each)

traditional Korean decorative motifs known as tae-geuks, which were meant to represent the five oceans and the five continents. They were arranged in a 'W' configuration meant to represent the first letter of the word 'World' in order to represent the harmony and unity of the disabled worldwide through sport. Their horizontal configuration represented equality and humanity, and the wave shape expressed the willingness and determination of the disabled to become fully active (IPC Newsletter, 2001a). Interestingly neither the Seoul Organising Committee nor the IPC make any mention of the colours used for the tae-geuks, nor the similarity of the logo to the IOC five rings logo and it was this that was to lead them into conflict with the IOC. The British Paralympic team for Seoul and the British Paralympic Association, formed in 1989, were amongst the first to incorporate the logo into their own (see Plate 2.1). However, sometime in 1990 the British Olympic Association contacted the IOC pointing out the similarity between the IPC logo and the IOC logo. This led to the IOC contacting the IPC in January 1991 to express their concerns that the five tae-geuk logo was confusingly similar to the Olympic symbol and requesting that IPC change their logo. The IOC Director of Legal Affairs, Howard M. Strupp made it clear that unless the

Plate 2.1 British Paralympic team logo for Seoul incorporating the five tae-geuk logo

matter was cleared up to the total satisfaction of the IOC a recommendation would be made to the IOC Executive Board with regard to sanctions to be taken by the IOC against IPC (IPC Newsletter, 2001b)

This left the IPC Executive Board in a very tricky situation as they were partly reliant on the funding that the IOC were now providing them with and in addition they did not want to jeopardise the working relationship they had recently forged. They, therefore, recommended a change in the logo 'in the spirit of co-operation' with the IOC. However, at the IPC General Assembly in Budapest in 1991 the member nations rejected a change of logo and decided to retain the current logo. The mood amongst the nations appears to have been that they felt they were being dictated to by the IOC rather than there being any kind of true co-operation on both sides. The decision of the general assembly did not go down well with the IOC or other National Olympic Committees worldwide, many of whom wrote to the IOC expressing their concerns over the impact this might have on marketing and sponsorship programmes. Following several meetings and negotiations with the IOC, the last of which occurred on 4 May 1992 the management committee of IPC concluded that they had no option other than to design a new logo, which they forwarded to the member nations for support and which was apparently, on the whole, favourably received (IPC Newsletter, 2002). However, it appears that some individuals were still not happy with the actions of the IOC and members of one national Paralympic team produced tee shirts that they intended to wear in protest at the Closing

Ceremony of the Barcelona Games in 1992 (see Plates 2.2 and 2.3). In the end their protest plans were discovered prior to the closing ceremony and they were prevented from carrying them out for fears of possible bad publicity that might ensue and the potential damage that might be caused to the relationship with the IOC. Given that the IOC had only really discovered the true value of their brand at the Los Angeles 1984 Games and had been extremely short of money prior to this their reaction is possibly understandable. However, it should be noted that these events occurred at a time when the social model of disability (see Chapter 4) was beginning to have a major impact on the disabled population, particularly in the West, and political activism in order to gain fair and equal access to society amongst the disabled community was becoming far more widespread.

Plate 2.2 Front of Barcelona protest tee-shirt

Plate 2.3 Reverse of Barcelona protest tee-shirt

Study activity

Do you think the International Paralympic Committee were right to back down and design a new logo? What do you think might have happened if they had kept with the five tae-geuks logo?

In the end the five tae-geuks logo was used at the Paralympic Games up to and including the Lillehammer Winter Paralympics of 1994 as it had already been used in advertising material for the Games prior to a final agreement being reached between the IOC and IPC.

Solidifying the closer working relationship between the IOC and IPC

Following the Lillehammer Winter Paralympic Games the IPC and IOC continued to co-operate with each other and the Paralympic Games continued to be hosted by the same host city as the Olympic Games. In the mid- to late 1990s in the wake of the Salt Lake City bidding scandal the IOC set up the IOC 2000 Commission on Ethics and Reform whose job it was to make recommendations aimed at reforming not only the bidding process, but also to try and repair some of the damage done to the image of the Olympic movement. As part of this process the then IPC President, Dr Robert Steadward, was one of only twelve individuals from outside the Olympic movement invited to sit on this commission. This appointment was the start of a much closer working relationship between the IOC and IPC, which culminated in two important events occurring at the Sydney 2000 Olympic and Paralympics Games. First, at the 111th IOC Session in Sydney, Dr Steadward was elected as an IOC member, thus strengthening the credibility and profile of the Paralympic movement. Then at the Sydney Paralympic Games Dr Steadward and Juan Antonio Samaranch, the then President of the IOC signed a general memorandum of understanding, which included representation of the IPC on IOC Commissions as well as financial assistance for the Paralympic movement from the IOC. This was followed about eight months later by the signing of a much more detailed co-operative agreement between the two organisations, dated 19 June 2001, which provided for the following benefits for the IPC and the Paralympic Games:

* a full seven years for the preparation of the Paralympic Games;
* full support of the host city and the OCOG for the organisation of the Paralympic Games;
* a financial guarantee of viability for the Paralympic Games;
* increased support for Paralympic athletes and team officials through travel grants, the elimination of entry fees and free provision of accommodation and ground transport;
* increased support for technical officials through free travel, accommodation and ground transport;
* support for the administration of the IPC.

(IOC-IPC Formal Agreement dated 19 June 2001)

Most of the proposals of this second agreement were not due to come into force until Beijing 2008. However, Athens 2004 and Turin 2006 voluntarily chose to implement many of the actions outlined in the agreement such as the concept of having a single organising committee for both Games. On 25 August 2003 the new Presidents of the two organisations, Dr Jacques Rogge (IOC) and Sir Philip Craven (IPC), signed an amendment to the 2001 agreement, which transferred broadcasting and marketing responsibilities of the 2008, 2010 and 2012 Paralympic Games to the host organising committees. In return the organising committees were to pay IPC US$9 million for the 2008 Games and US$14 million for the 2010 and 2012 Games.

Study activity

What are the possible reasons that the IOC might enter into such agreements with the IPC? What possible benefits might the IOC accrue from such an agreement?

Conclusion

Knowing what is known now about the size and success of the Paralympic Games and where they have grown from it would not be an understatement to describe Ludwig Guttmann as a visionary. His claims in 1949 that the Stoke Mandeville Games would one day become recognised as the paraplegic's equivalent of the Olympic Games appeared laughable at the time, but events have proved him correct. The relationship between the IOC and the international disability sports movement has been quite turbulent at times, but overall the growing relationship between the two organisations has had an extremely positive impact on the growth and success of the Paralympic Games.

Chapter review questions

1   Outline the impact of Dr Guttmann's attempts to constantly link the Stoke Mandeville Games to the Olympic Games and his reason for doing so.
2   Describe the IOC's reaction to the use of Olympic terminology and the use of the five tae guks symbol by the disability sports movement. Do you think the reaction of the IOC was the correct one?
3   Outline the impact the return to Olympics host cities and the closer working relationship with IOC have had on the Paralympic Games.

Suggested further reading

Bailey, S., 2008, *Athlete First: A History of the Paralympic Movement*, John Wiley & Sons Ltd, Chichester, UK.

Brittain, I., 2008, *The Evolution of the Paralympic Games*, in Cashman, R. and Darcy. S., Benchmark Games: The Sydney 2000 Paralympic Games, Walla Walla Press, Petersham, NSW, pp. 19–34.

3 The governance of Paralympic sport

Chapter aims

- Outline the development of the organisational structure for international disability sport and the Paralympic Games.
- Describe the current aims of the International Paralympic Committee as contained in their strategic plan.
- Outline the current administrative structure for international disability sport and the International Paralympic Committee.

As outlined in Chapter 1 disability sport from an organisational perspective originally developed along the lines of specific impairment groups. Originally there were six of these International Organisations of Sport for the Disabled (IOSDs), but in 2002 the International Stoke Mandeville Wheelchair Sports Federation (ISMWSF) merged with the International Sports Organisation for the Disabled (ISOD) to form the International Wheelchair and Amputee Sports Federation (IWAS). Therefore, the five current IOSDs are:

- The International Wheelchair and Amputee Sports Federation (IWAS)
- The International Blind Sports Association (IBSA)
- The Cerebral Palsied International Sports and Recreation Association (CP-ISRA)
- The International Sports Federation for People with an Intellectual Disability (INAS-FID)
- The Comité International des Sports des Sourds (CISS)

The first three are currently members of IPC and take part in the Paralympic Games. INAS-FID are also members of IPC, however, their athletes are currently banned from the Paralympic Games. The reasons behind this can be found in Chapter 10. CISS, who are responsible for deaf and hard of hearing athletes have their own world games called the Deaflympics, which usually take place the year following the Paralympic Summer and Winter Games. Today each IOSD is responsible for the development of sport for athletes in the specific impairment groups that they represent. Each organisation has its own world games, although with IWAS, IBSA and CP-ISRA these Games are largely a stepping stone for athletes wishing to make the Paralympic Games, as well as an opportunity to experience international competition for those athletes who may never be quite good enough to perform at the Paralympic Games.

The International Paralympic Committee acts as an umbrella body to co-ordinate Paralympic sport at both the Paralympic Games and at IPC multi-disability World Championship level. World championships for sports that are that are specific to a particular impairment group (e.g. judo for the blind) are organised by the relevant IOSD (e.g. IBSA), but where a sport (e.g. Athletics), includes athletes from a variety of the IOSDs then IPC are responsible. Before going any further it is worth recounting how and why this situation came about.

Towards a single worldwide organisational body for international disability sport

The gradual breaking up of the International Sports Organisation for the Disabled (ISOD) into three separate organisations (CP-ISRA, IBSA, ISOD) in the late 1970s and early 1980s led Sir Ludwig to raise the question at the ISOD General Assembly in Madrid in March, 1977, as to exactly what the future role of ISOD should be. This led to the preparation of a discussion document, presented in November, 1978 by Joan Scruton, Secretary General of ISOD and ISMGF. In it she raised the possibility of ISOD taking on the role of an overall umbrella organisation that would become the co-ordinating committee for sport for all disabled and in Olympic years would act as an overall organising body representing all the relevant individual sports organisations. This is something the IOC had also been pushing for in its dealings with the disability sport movement as its representatives found it quite confusing trying to deal with such a wide variety of organisations.

Following a report in April 1979 by Guillermo Cabezas, Vice President of ISOD, and Ariel Fink, Vice President of ISMGF, on the setting up of a single federation a study group was set up consisting of representatives from all interested parties. The group held three meetings in July 1979, June 1980 (Arnhem), and December 1980 (Stoke Mandeville), which came up with several drafts of ideas for a new organisation. In the end the recommendations of the study group were rejected. However, it was recognised that the united efforts of the different disability organisations represented within the study group were the basis for further mutual co-operation. Therefore, at the ISOD General Assembly in December 1981, the new President of ISOD, following the death of Sir Ludwig, Mr Avronsaart, invited the three other international sports organisations involved in the Paralympic Games to a meeting in order to discuss the establishment of a Co-operative Committee.

With the International Blind Sports Association (IBSA) having been founded in Paris in 1981, there were four different International Organisations for Sport for the Disabled (IOSDs) represented at the founding meeting on 11

March 1982 in Leysin, Switzerland during the Second World Championships in Winter Sports for the Disabled:

- International Stoke Mandeville Games Federation (ISMGF)
- International Sports Organisation for the Disabled (ISOD)
- International Blind Sports Association (IBSA) (1981)
- Cerebral Palsied – International Sports and Recreation Association (CP-ISRA) (1978)

After lengthy discussion it was unanimously agreed that the four international organisations should form a co-operative committee, with the chairmanship of future meetings of this co-operative committee rotating amongst the Presidents of the four member organisations. At the second meeting of the committee on 28 July 1982 at Stoke Mandeville it was agreed that the name for the new co-operative committee should be the International Co-ordinating Committee (ICC). This was later amended at the fifth meeting of ICC in 1984 to the International Co-ordinating Committee of World Sports Organisations for the Disabled. At the tenth meeting held in Gothenburg, Sweden in August 1986 the Comité International des Sports des Sourds (CISS), representing the deaf, and the International Association of Sports for Persons with a Mental Handicap (INAS-FMH) were accepted into membership of ICC.

ICC and national representation

Following an ICC seminar held in the Netherlands in February 1985 recommendations were made that a further seminar be held, to which national members were invited, in order to discuss a possible future structure of ICC to include national representation. This seminar was finally held in Arnhem, the Netherlands from 12–15 March 1987. As well as representation from the six IOSDs the seminar was also attended by representatives from thirty-nine voting countries and 106 national and international disability sports organisations in total. The main recommendation to come out of the seminar was that there had to be a change in the existing ICC structure and that any future structure must include: first, national representation, second, representation from and the continued existence of the IOSDs, third, regional representation and finally, representation from the athletes. An *ad hoc* committee was appointed to formulate a constitution for the new organisation to replace ICC. It was voted that the *ad hoc* committee should consist of the six representatives of the IOSDs, one elected representative from each of the Continental Associations and three athlete representatives. The new constitution proposed by them was circulated to the member nations and then discussed at a hearing during the Seoul Paralympic Summer Games in 1988. The hearing that occurred in Seoul was actually a very turbulent and highly charged affair with many representatives actually leaving the meeting, partly in frustration. However, it was finally agreed that

draft recommendations for the new constitution should be submitted to the
ad hoc committee by 21 December 1988 and that a final draft constitution
would be circulated to national and international organisations by 1 March
1989. This final draft was finally discussed and voted upon at a General
Assembly held in Dusseldorf, Germany on 21–22 September 1989.

The formation of the International Paralympic Committee

The General Assembly in Dusseldorf did not start well for the IOSDs when
it was decided that only national organisations had the right to speak and
vote. However, after some strenuous lobbying from the floor the decision
was overturned and the IOSDs were finally given both speaking and voting
rights. Part of the reason for these initial problems was possibly the fact that
a neutral Chairperson, Dr Wilf Preising, was selected to chair the assembly,
but lacked knowledge and experience of the political rivalries inherent
within international disability sport at the time. There followed many hours
of, sometimes acrimonious, debate and argument and just when it appeared
that an agreement would never be reached a series of motions from the
floor by Jens Bromann (Denmark), York Chow (Hong Kong) and André Raes
(Belgium) enabled the assembly to come to an agreement. Originally the new
organisation was to have been called the International Confederation of Sports
Organisations for the Disabled (ICSOD), but following a vote it was decided
that it should be called the International Paralympic Committee (IPC) instead.
The key objective of the newly formed IPC was decreed as being the only
world multi-disability organisation with the right to organise Paralympic and
multi-disability World Games, as well as World Championships. Following a
further vote the structure of the proposed executive committee was enlarged
from twenty to twenty-three members with the addition of an extra regional
representative, splitting Asia into east and west, a Technical Officer and a
Medical Officer. Prior to voting for the new Executive Board it was decreed
that no one standing for a position could, if elected, also hold a position
on the Executive Board of one of the IOSDs. This ruling caused several
candidates to withdraw from the elections. The six IOSDs and the forty-one
countries that were represented by various NOSD's are recognised as the
founding members of the International Paralympic Committee. These were:

Australia	Austria	Belgium	Bulgaria	Canada
Cyprus	Czechoslovakia	Denmark	Egypt	Faroe Isles
Finland	France	Germany	Greece	Hong Kong
Hungary	Iceland	Iran	Iraq	Ireland
Israel	Italy	Jordan	Kenya	Korea
Kuwait	Luxembourg	Malta	Morocco	Netherlands
New Zealand	Norway	Poland	Portugal	Spain
Sweden	Switzerland	USSR	UK	USA
Venezuela				

The ICC – IPC handover of responsibilities

IPC held their first Executive Committee meeting in Duisburg, Germany on 23 September 1989, the day after the General Assembly had closed. One of their first orders of business was to inform the IOC, ICC and the United Nations (UN) of their existence and objectives. With the contracts already signed by ICC for the Winter and Summer Paralympic Games to be held in Tignes, Barcelona and Madrid in 1992, IPC were unsure exactly as to when full authority should be passed from ICC to IPC. At the first ICC meeting held after the General Assembly in January 1990 in Barcelona the general consensus was that the meeting in Dusseldorf had been very badly organised and chaotic and that a large part of the world, in particular the Far East and South Pacific Regions, had had no opportunity to vote. However, both the IPC Executive and ICC meetings agreed that there should be reciprocal invitations for members of each organisation to attend each other's meetings in order to facilitate the transfer. Indeed, after some initial discussion the new President and Secretary General of IPC, Bob Steadward and André Raes, were invited to join the ICC meeting in Barcelona. After two sessions of discussion regarding the outcomes of Dusseldorf it was voted on and agreed that the transition of responsibility from ICC to IPC would be postponed until the first meeting of ICC after the General Assembly of IPC held in conjunction with the Assen World Games for the Disabled in June 1990. In the meantime ICC was to extend an invitation to the President and Secretary General of IPC to attend ICC meetings as observers. At the second IPC General Assembly, which was held in Groningen rather than Assen, it was proposed by Jens Bromann, President of IBSA, that an agreement be drawn up between ICC and IPC regarding the transfer of authority. A meeting was held between the six Presidents of the IOSDs and the IPC President on 5 October 1990 in Aylesbury, UK to draw up the agreement and it was signed the next day by all concerned at the eighteenth meeting of ICC. The outcome of the agreement was that ICC would continue to be responsible for the 1992 Winter and Summer Paralympic Games, but that from that day forward IPC would assume immediate control over all other world multi-disability (more than one IOSD) games. On completion of the 1992 Paralympic Games ICC and IPC would then issue a joint communiqué spelling out the final transfer of power from ICC to IPC. Following the successful completion of the Winter and Summer Paralympic Games of 1992, ICC held their twenty-third and final meeting at the Sandy Beach Hotel, Larnaca, Cyprus from 24–25 March 1993. At the meeting Jens Bromann moved that all residual funds after the winding up of ICC should be transferred to IPC. The motion was seconded by Bob Steadward, President of IPC. Although the motion was lost, after some discussion Bob Steadward proposed that each of the IOSDs (CP-ISRA, IBSA, ISMWSF, and ISOD) receive 10,000 dollars with the remainder being transferred to IPC. INAS-FMH were not to receive the payment as they were in debt to ICC for a similar amount for sanction fees from the Madrid Games. This motion passed with a majority of five in favour and one against.

In 2006 IPC published its strategic plan to cover the period 2006–2009. Its overall vision is to enable Paralympic athletes to achieve sporting excellence and inspire and excite the world. In order to achieve this vision the strategic plan encompasses five strategic objectives developed in co-operation with the management team and the IPC committees, which must be successfully delivered in order to achieve this mission. These objectives are as follows:

1   To be a *high performing organisation*. The IPC is a high performing democratic sporting organisation that abides by its values and is dedicated to excellence. In order to ensure that this is maintained and improved upon IPC needs to be an efficient organisation with a clear governance structure and concise strategic direction, which supports reliable operations.

2   To facilitate *membership development* in order to ensure that all IPC member organisations are active, self-sustainable and deliver quality services within their respective roles within the Paralympic Movement. In order to achieve this, IPC must ensure that its member organisations have defined roles and responsibilities, are able to sustain their operations and are accountable and effective when delivering their activities.

3   Improve *resource creation* by ensuring IPC has a solid and sustainable human and financial foundation that ensures its long-term viability, which will ensure that IPC is an effective and well-resourced organisation that is able to meet its objectives and the needs of all its members.

4   To ensure Paralympic Games *success* by ensuring that the Games are a viable, sustainable and distinctive sporting experience that inspires and excites the world. This should result in a sporting event with a clear and comprehensive identity with services that are of the highest quality and are sport and athlete focused.

5   To achieve *global recognition* by ensuring that the Paralympic brand is defined and globally recognised, understood and valued, resulting in a brand that has defined attributes and clear messages that is recognised in the sporting environment, instantly understood by the general public and the media and valued by partners.

(IPC Strategic Plan, 2006)

The structure of IPC has grown and changed beyond all recognition since its creation in 1989, which is a clear reflection of the growth that has occurred in both the Paralympic Movement and the organisation necessary to maintain it. Overleaf is a structural diagram of the current general structure of IPC showing the various groups that have a stake in the running of the movement (see Figure 3.1).

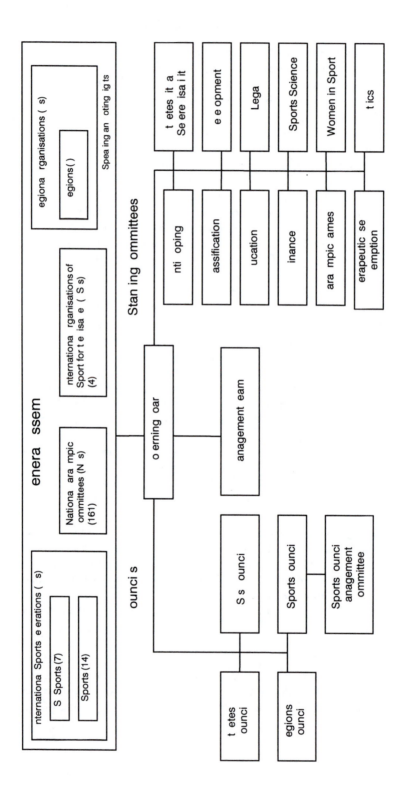

Figure 3.1 International Paralympic Committee Governance Structure

General Assembly

The IPC General Assembly is held every two years in the year between the Summer and Winter Paralympic Games. It is the highest decision making authority of the International Paralympic Committee and consists of all member groups that make up IPC, which are as follows:

Sports

Paralympic Sports are classified into three groups dependent upon who has overall organisational responsibility for them at the Paralympic Games.

IPC sports

An IPC Sport is a multi-disability sport for athletes with a disability governed by the IPC under the management of an IPC Sports Committee. There are currently eight IPC Sports on the Paralympic Programme and one other IPC Sport, not on the Paralympic Programme, but whose Championship Programme (e.g. World and Regional Championships) is managed by IPC.

IPC sports in the paralympic programme

Summer Sports:	Winter Sports:
Powerlifting	Alpine Skiing
Shooting	Cross-Country Skiing
Swimming	Ice Sledge Hockey
Athletics	Biathlon

Other IPC Sports (not on Paralympic programme): Wheelchair Dance Sport

IOSD sports

An IOSD Sport is a sport for athletes with a disability on the Paralympic Programme governed by an IOSD. There are currently seven such sports on the Paralympic programme.

CP-ISRA:	Boccia	IBSA:	Football 5-a-side
	Football 7-a-side		Goalball
			Judo
IWAS:	Wheelchair fencing		
	Wheelchair rugby		

Independent Paralympic sports federations

An Independent Paralympic Sports Federation (IPSF) is an independent sport federation recognised by IPC as the sole world-wide representative of a sport for athletes with a disability that has been granted the status as a Paralympic Sport by IPC. There are currently ten federations recognised by IPC that have sports on the Paralympic programme:

Summer Games

Federation Internationale de Tir a L'Arc (FITA): (Archery)
Union Cyclisme Internationale (UCI): (Cycling)
Fédération Equestre Internationale (FEI): (Equestrian)
Fédération Internationale des Sociétés d'Aviron (FISA): (Rowing)
The International Federation for Disabled Sailing (IFDS): (Sailing)
The International Table Tennis Federation (ITTF): (Table tennis)
The International Wheelchair Basketball Federation (IWBF): (Wheelchair basketball)
The International Tennis Federation (ITF): (Wheelchair tennis)
The World Organization Volleyball for the Disabled (WOVD): (Sitting volleyball)

Winter Games

The World Curling Federation (WCF): (Wheelchair curling)

Other IPSF Sports (not on the Paralympic programme)
International Bowls for the Disabled (IBD): (Bowls)

In terms of the Paralympic Games the function of an IPSF is to exercise technical jurisdiction and guidance over the competition and training venues of its respective sport during the Games.

Study activity

What kinds of issues might arise when a particular sport for people with disabilities (e.g. archery) is integrated into the structure of the non-disabled International Federation for that sport (e.g. FITA)?

Regional organisations

A regional organisation is an independent regional organisation recognised as the sole regional representative of the IPC members within a specific region as defined by the IPC. The IPC currently recognizes three regional organisations:

The African Sports Confederation of Disabled (Africa): (www.ascod.org)

The European Paralympic Committee (Europe): (www.europaralympic.org)
The Oceania Paralympic Committee (Oceania): (No website at present)

Until such time as an independent regional organisation is created, the IPC has established two further regional committees to act as the sole representative body in that region:

The Paralympic Committee of the Americas (Americas):
(www.americasparalympic.org)
The Asian Paralympic Committee (Asia): (www.asianparalympic.org)

The role of regional organisations is to liaise with IPC on behalf of its members in the respective region, organise regional sports events, co-ordinate their development activities with IPC and provide support to the IPC membership within the respective region.

National Paralympic Committees

A National Paralympic Committee (NPC) is a national organisation recognised by IPC as the sole representative of athletes with a disability in that country or territory to IPC. IPC currently has 161 National Paralympic Committees in membership.

Africa	41 NPCs
The Americas	25 NPCs
Asia	40 NPCs
Europe	48 NPCs.
Oceania	7 NPCs

The role of an NPC is to undertake the co-ordination and support of IPC activities and Paralympic Sport within their respective territory. They are also responsible for the entrance, management and team preparation for the Paralympic Games and other IPC sanctioned competitions.

Study activity

Find out what you can about the NPC in your own country. How does it fit into the overall sporting structure of your country and how do you think things might be changed or improved to increase the chances of future success by your nation's Paralympic athletes?

International organisations of sport for the disabled

An International Organisation of Sport for the Disabled (IOSD) is an independent organisation recognised by IPC as the sole representative of a specific impairment group to IPC. IOSDs co-operate with IPC in providing the impairment specific expertise required to develop sport for athletes with a disability from the grass roots level to elite level. They also co-ordinate their development activities with IPC. As stated in previous chapters IPC currently recognises four IOSDs:

The Cerebral Palsy International Sports and Recreation Association (CP-ISRA)

The aim of CP-ISRA is to promote and develop the means by which people who have cerebral palsy or a related neurological condition throughout the world can have access to opportunities for participation in sport and recreational activities of their choice and to encourage and facilitate the organisation and running of world, national and regional games. Their headquarters are in Bad Neuenahr-Ahrweiler, Germany (www.cpisra.org).

The International Blind Sports Federation (IBSA)

Founded in Paris in 1981, IBSA is registered as a non-profit making, public interest body based in Spain, that encourages and provides opportunities for all blind and visually impaired people to get involved in different sports and physical activities. Their headquarters are in Madrid (www.ibsa.es).

The International Wheelchair and Amputee Sports Federation (IWAS)

IWAS was formed in 2002 from the merger between the International Stoke Mandeville Wheelchair Sports Federation (ISMWSF) and the International Sports Organisation for the Disabled (ISOD). Its aim is to enable the growth and achievements of persons with a physical disability in sport and provide opportunities to achieve individual aspirations at all levels through a defined athlete pathway. Their headquarters are at Stoke Mandeville (www.iwasf.com).

The International Sports Federation for Persons with an Intellectual Disability (INAS-FID)

INAS-FID was founded in 1986 and is responsible for providing sporting opportunities for athletes with intellectual disabilities who wish to take part in open competitive sport performed under the rules of the relevant International Federation. The aims of INAS-FID are different from, and should not be confused with, Special Olympics who also cater for athletes with an intellectual disability. Please see Chapter 10 for further details. Their headquarters are in Wakefield, UK (www.inas-fid.org).

Governing Board

The Governing Board is the representative of the IPC Membership, elected at the General Assembly in accordance with nomination and election procedures adopted by the IPC Membership at the 2004 Extraordinary General Assembly. It is responsible for overseeing the affairs of IPC in between meetings of the General Assembly and comprises fifteen members, including one President, one Vice-President, ten Members-at-Large, one co-opted member (member without vote), one Athletes' representative (ex-officio member with vote, elected by the Athletes' Council) and the CEO (ex-officio member without vote). The Governing Board is chaired by the President and holds meetings at least three times a year. It is primarily responsible for the implementation of policies and directions set by the General Assembly. Additionally, the Governing Board provides recommendations on membership, including conditions for membership and fees, to the General Assembly as well as recommendations on motions received from members. It is also responsible for approving budgets and audited accounts, IPC Rules and Regulations, membership of IPC Committees and the Paralympic Games.

Councils

Athletes' Council

The Athletes' Council is the collective voice of Paralympic athletes within IPC and the greater Paralympic Movement. It acts as the liaison between IPC decision-makers and Paralympic athletes and works to provide effective input into decision-making at all levels of the organisation. A member of the IPC Athletes' Council also sits on the IOC Athletes' Commission. The IPC Athlete's Council consists of nine Paralympic athlete representatives elected for a four-year term. Six athlete representatives are elected from summer sports and three from winter sports at the Paralympic Games. Athlete candidates are nominated by their respective National Paralympic Committee and must have competed at a Paralympic Games within the previous eight years. The Athletes' Council meets at least once a year at the invitation of the Chairperson and upon request of the IPC Governing Board. Its roles include overseeing the Athletes' Council election process during the Paralympic Games to ensure that they are organised in a democratic and fair manner and aim to ensure maximum participation by athletes eligible to vote. Successful candidates are announced during the Closing Ceremony of the respective Paralympic Games.

Regions' Council

The IPC Regions' Council provides feedback, advice and representation on the IPC Governing Board on behalf of and in the interests of their respective regions in all IPC matters. It consists of representatives from each of the five regional organisations mentioned above and provides a forum for the exchange of information on matters of common interest. It advises the Governing Board in relevant matters and assists in the development of IPC Policies and the Strategic plan.

IOSDs' Council

The IPC IOSDs' Council provides feedback, advice and reports to the IPC Governing Board, on behalf of and in the interests of their respective athletes and officials in all IPC matters. It consists of representatives of each of the four IOSDs mentioned above. The Council provides a forum for exchange of information on matters of common interest. It advises the Governing Board in relevant matters and assists in the development of IPC Policies and the Strategic plan.

Sports Council

The IPC Sports Council provides feedback, advice and reports to the IPC Governing Board, on behalf of and in the interest of sports recognised by the IPC. The Sports Council provides an annual forum for exchange of information on matters of common interest, sharing of best practices and expertise within and between the Sports. It currently comprises thirty-two members representing each sport on the Paralympic Programme, two non-Paralympic Programme IPC Sports, each IOSD, the Athletes, as well as specific IPC Governing Board positions (i.e. Medical Officer, Summer Sports Representative). The Sports Council meets at least once a year and advises the IPC Governing Board in the development of IPC Policies in general, and on appropriate policies for the Paralympic Games. The Sports Council also provides consultation to the IPC Management Team in the development of the strategic direction in relation to Paralympic sports.

Standing committees

There are currently twelve standing committees (see Figure 3.1) which were established to consult and advise IPC on a variety of issues pertinent to the running of both the Paralympic Games and the organisation as a whole. Members are nominated from within the member organisations and then selected by the Governing Board.

IPC Management Team

The IPC Management Team consists of the professional staff working under the direction of the Chief Executive Officer (CEO). With the authority delegated by the Governing Board, the CEO represents the Governing Board and IPC in all day-to-day business affairs.

Conclusion

As the size and success of the Paralympic Games and international disability sport in general has grown the complexity and size of the structure necessary for it to continue to grow and succeed has grown accordingly. This brings with it many issues that need to be addressed or overcome. A number of these issues will be outlined within the remaining chapters of this book.

Chapter review questions

1   Name the five IOSDs currently in existence and describe their role in international disability sport.
2   What is the role of the International Paralympic Committee in international disability sport?
3   List the five key objectives of the IPC Strategic Plan.
4   What is the role of a National Paralympic Committee (NPC)? How much do you know about the NPC in your area.

Suggested further reading

DePauw, K. and Gavron, S.J., 2005, *Disability Sport* (2nd edn), Human Kinetics, Leeds, UK.

4 Disability and the body

Chapter aims

- Outline the medical, social and bio-social models of disability and their relevance.
- Review the place of disability in relation to concepts such as normality and oppression.
- Review the role of language and its impact upon people with disabilities.

How any group of people get on in life is very often dependent upon how that group is viewed and treated by the rest of society. This first section outlines the ways people with disabilities have been viewed throughout history and the way these views have been perceived and interpreted by individuals and groups working in disability research. DePauw (1997) highlights the importance of people's perceptions and definitions of the body and their effect on perceptions of disability and argues that:

> An understanding of the body, our attitudes toward the body, ... is important because how we view the body and how we define sport impacts how we view disability and individuals with disabilities.
>
> (DePauw, 1997, p. 420)

According to Dunn and Sherrill (1996) some, although they don't say whom, have argued that society, in its attempts to try and understand people with disabilities, has progressed or evolved through a series of phases in its treatment of the disabled. However, it should be noted that they appear to be talking about western society in particular. They summarise these phases thus:

Extermination

This has occurred throughout history from ancient times for a variety of reasons including some religious beliefs that held that people with disabilities were evil, to modern genetic engineers who put a modern spin on the need to exterminate anything that might interfere with ideal or 'normal' development of the human body, for example Nazi Germany (See also Morris, 1991, pp. 51–8).

Ridicule

Earlier societies, particularly in the medieval period where many of the court jesters were individuals with different appearances or mental functions (e.g. dwarfs, hunchbacks), were prone to ridicule and taunt those who were disabled in some way. Even today individuals with disabilities frequently have to endure rude, ignorant and offensive comments. Our language is full of expressions that have a tendency to poke fun at those with disabilities (for example cripple, retarded) (see also Shearer, 1981, p. 5).

Institutionalisation

Up to the early 1900s, it was very common to institutionalise any individual who somehow deviated significantly from the norm. Although this was viewed as the humane thing to do, many acknowledge that institutions were created to protect the able-bodied from those with disabilities (see also Barnes, 1991, pp. 15–20).

Education

In more modern times, more recent views of those with disabilities have helped some within society to understand that educating these individuals leads to productive citizens. To a large extent, however, those with disabilities continue to lag far behind in overall education and this lack of adequate education affects employment, income and independence (see also Barnes, 1991, pp. 20–2).

Self-realisation

According to Dunn and Sherrill (1996), individuals with disabilities are increasingly accepted as individuals without focusing on, or generalising about, their disability. They claim this is evident, for instance, in efforts to promote programmes that integrate people with disabilities into all facets of life, including schools, employment, and recreation. To a large extent, however, individuals with disabilities are still viewed by many as a 'class or category' with little appreciation or understanding of the unique nature of each person, regardless of the disability. This is an argument that many writers in the field of disability concur with (Swain *et al.*, 1993; Barnes, 1991; Shearer, 1981). According Dunn and Sherrill (1996), this tendency to categorise all individuals with disabilities, or to stereotype, is a particularly hurtful type of prejudice that further contributes to the depersonalisation of individuals with disabilities.

Disability, definitions and societal perceptions

All of the historical phases of treatment of people with disabilities introduced above are based upon the prevalent societal perceptions of disability and people with disabilities at that time. How disability is defined within a particular society potentially says a lot about how that society perceives disability and people with disabilities. Below are three definitions of the term 'disability' which clearly pathologise disability, that is represent it as biologically situated and produced:

1   Disability: The   loss   or   reduction   of   functional   ability. (World Health Organisation (1980) in DePauw (1997, p. 422))
2   Disability, *noun* – 1. The state of being disabled. 2. A condition such as a physical handicap that results in partial or complete loss of a person's ability to perform social, occupational or other everyday activities. (Chambers Encyclopaedic English Dictionary (1994, p. 365) Larousse PLC, Edinburgh)
3   Disability, *n.* – 1. A physical incapacity; either congenital or caused by injury, disease, etc., esp. when limiting a person's ability to work. 2. A lack of some asset, quality, or attribute, that prevents a person from doing something.

(Oxford Illustrated Dictionary (1998, p. 230)
Oxford University Press, Oxford)

These definitions of disability form the basis for what constitutes conventional views of disability. DePauw (1997), Oliver (1993b) and Morris (1991) have pointed to the ways in which such taken for granted notions identify individual impairment as the problem, placing this problem squarely on the shoulders of the individual with a disability. This is termed the medical model of disability. It has as its emphasis a disability – specific or categorical approach that reinforces and perpetuates the perspective of disability as found in the person and their individual impairment and, therefore, as a problem of the individual (Brown and Smith, 1989).

Power – knowledge, medical model discourse and disability

A key concept in defining how powerful ideas shape or generate a framework of discipline for organisational systems is the Foucauldian idea of power-knowledge. This is based on common assumptions and according to Foucault these assumptions underlie particular patterns of language use, particularly in 'expert jargon' (O'Donnell, 1997, p. 98). Foucault calls a set of common assumptions related to a particular topic a 'discourse', which according to Layder (1994):

refers to all that can be thought, written or said about a particular thing such as a product (like a car, or a washing detergent), or a topic of specialist knowledge (such as sport or medicine). In this sense, the ability to employ a discourse reflects a command of knowledge of a particular area. It also implies that this facility is employed in relation to people who lack such command and have no legitimate claim to such knowledge. For instance, command of a particular discourse, such as that of medicine or law, also allows control over those who do not, such as patients and clients.

(Layder, 1994, p. 97)

According to O'Donnell (1997) those who do have command over the knowledge within a particular discourse, the experts, have the power or authority to establish that discourse, which can then be extremely difficult to challenge without the help of an alternative set of experts. In modern day western societies the power of the medical profession, gained through its ability to both define and name illnesses and body parts as well as the power to heal injuries and cure illnesses, has put them in a very strong position to create and perpetuate discourses with respect to many areas of life related to the body and mind including disability. Along with this power to define comes 'control and discipline' (O'Donnell, 1997, p. 99). The medical profession work from a biological perspective and this has led to disability being conceived of as merely a biological product. Therefore, the general view is that the problems that face people with disabilities are the result of their physical and/or intellectual impairments and are independent of the wider socio-cultural, physical, and political environments. The power of the medical profession within society has played a significant role in creating many of the societal perceptions of disability that are embedded within the medical model discourse. A large part of the reason for this, according to Wendell (1996), is that:

Their authority operates far beyond medical institutions – inside and in relation to government bureaucracies, insurance companies, courts, schools, charities, rehabilitative organizations, and institutes for long-term care. Medical professionals also exercise considerable authority with all types of employers, certifying people medically capable or incapable of working.

(Wendell, 1996, p. 117)

As a result of this 'cognitive authority' of the medical profession (Addelson, 1983, cited in Wendell, 1996, p. 117) both the non-disabled and people with disabilities within society are strongly encouraged, through the numerous, apparently legitimate, sources (such as those described by Wendell, above) in which they encounter it, to 'internalise' many of the perceptions of disability embedded in the medical model approach to disability. Consequently, it appears to people with disabilities that the cause of many of their problems lie within them and their impairments. In addition this powerful and apparently 'legitimised' discourse is then taken up and used by other organisations and institutions within society to inform policy or to exert power over those with disabilities, that is, a particular understanding of disability has been normalised within society. Therefore, those with the most legitimate claim to determine and define the discourse in the area of disability (people who actually have disabilities) are strongly encouraged to accept a discourse that is not in their best interests. But because the rest of society has also internalised such a discourse and, as such, accepts disability as pathological (that is, based on biology), it has become almost impossible for them to put forward an alternative discourse that will be listened to.

Drake (1999), by way of an explanation for the position of people with disabilities within British society, introduces the work of Lukes (1974) and his three dimensional analysis of power. Drake states that, first, for Lukes, power is an active concept, the direct exercise of which might take the form of decision-making or by the use of force or imposition of authority. In the case of disability one such authority would be that of the medical profession as discussed above, who have the power not only to label someone as 'disabled' but also the power to affect their access to assistance to cope with the disability such as state benefits. Drake (1999) states that in Lukes' second dimension of power he introduces the notion of 'deliberate non-decision', which includes the ideas in the first dimension and which results in the suppression or thwarting of a latent or manifest challenge to the values or interests of the decision maker. Insofar as the inactivity is deliberate, this is an exercise of power. Reasons for this may include issues such as cost. It is cheaper to label someone as 'disabled' and give them benefits than it would be to admit that it might actually be other factors such as the built environment that disables them and pay to have that environment made accessible. In terms of disability this might be one possible reason to explain why proponents of the social model of disability (outlined in the next section) find it so hard to gain acceptance for their ideas, although the overall reason is likely to be far more complex. According to Drake (1999) Lukes' third and final dimension is most closely related to the ideas of Gramsci's hegemony theory in which Gramsci (1971) states 'the ascendancy of a class or group rests on its ability to translate its own worldview into a pervasive dominant ethos' (Gramsci 1971 cited in Drake, 1999, p. 14). Drake states that in Lukes' view this involves the shaping of people's perceptions, cognitions and preferences in such a way that they accept their role in the existing order because they can neither see nor imagine an alternative to it. However, as Burr (1995, p. 71) states 'if people really understood that they were being controlled they would not stand for it.' As a possible explanation for this situation Burr cites Foucault (1976) who claims "power is tolerable only on condition that it mask a substantial part of itself. Its success is proportional to its ability to hide its own mechanisms" (Foucault, 1976 cited in Burr, 1995, p.71).

In the case of disability this power is successfully hidden, through the perceptions embedded in the medical model of disability, by transferring the 'blame' for an individual's situation on to the individual with a disability, thus forcing them to accept a situation that is not in their best interests. This is then reinforced by regular reference to societal norms and because people with disabilities do not fit into these norms, for example, they get around using a wheelchair instead of walking or cannot see as well as the majority of society, this leads to the situation of people with disabilities being taken for granted by most members of society. Although it is difficult to discern this situation from a situation of genuine consensus, Lukes suggests that where power is exercised by means of a social construction of reality there will exist 'latent conflict' (Lukes, 1971 cited in Drake, 1999, p.15). In the case of disability there is a contradiction between those exercising power and the 'real interests' of those they exclude through the imposition of the perceptions of disability embedded in the medical model discourse and it is up to those who are excluded to discover what their 'real interests' are and act.

Some academics have attempted to redefine this discourse, in conjunction with people with disabilities, in order to try and gain legitimacy for the arguments contained within the social model of disability, within the eyes of the rest of society. This is an approach that several scholars, also within the fields of sport and physical education, now appear to be advocating. DePauw (2000, p. 365) claims that co-operation with people with disabilities 'can help move our research and scholarship from studies of disability as a biological category to the understanding of disability as a social identity' and Barton (1993, p. 52) whilst discussing the issues of 'rights, choice, power and change' in reference to the emancipatory process within school physical education states 'part of this process involves the participation of disabled people in those decisions affecting their lives and over which they have expert knowledge'.

Study Activity

List some of the names you have heard used as insults thrown at individuals who have played particularly badly in a sporting activity. How many of them relate to disability or specific impairments? Discuss the link between these insults and what they might tell us about perceptions of disability and disability sport.

The social model of disability

According to Morris (1991) in recent years, many of those involved in the disability movement have argued against the perceptions of disability embedded in the medical model, which health and social services professionals (and the general public) tend to apply to people with disabilities. Disability activists have, therefore, developed a social model of disability, arguing that it is environmental barriers and social attitudes that disable. According to Devine (1997, p.4) social construction theory 'seeks to explain the process by which knowledge is created and assumed as reality.' In terms of disability and the use of the social model by disability activists to fight against the dominant perceptions of disability, based upon a medical model ethos, within society, Priestley (1998) claims its use has its roots in the work of the Union of Physically Impaired Against Segregation (UPIAS) (1976) and Vic Finkelstein (1980), both in Great Britain. These works 'form the core assumptions' for modern day contributors in this area (Priestley, 1998, p. 80). Morris (1991) states that this perspective takes the view that if people's attitudes were to change, and there was public policy that legislated that environmental barriers should be removed, then many of the problems associated with disability would disappear. This view is exemplified in the comments of Drake (1996, cited in Imrie, 1997):

> disablement lies in the construction of society, not in the physical condition of the individual. However, this argument is usually rejected precisely because to accept it involves recognising the extent to which we are not merely unfortunate but are directly oppressed by a hostile social environment.
>
> (Drake, 1996, cited in Imrie, 1997, p. 263)

The bio-social model of disability

However, Imrie (1997) himself argues strongly against this perspective. He claims that this perspective suggests that a change in the physical environment (access to buildings, etc.) can change the experiences of people with disabilities. However, such transformations alone will do little or nothing to destroy the underlying disablist values within society or the institutional structures within which people with disabilities are forced to operate. He claims that the reverse is, in fact, more likely:

> because such perspectives (social model of disability) de-politicise the very essence of 'being disabled' as either an individual condition or one connected to the policy practices of policy institutions. Wider structural conditions are lost sight of while the body is conceived of (if at all) as ephemeral.
>
> (Imrie, 1997, p. 270)

This attempt to include impairment within the overall understanding of disability and its impact within a society is known as the bio-social model. What this appears to indicate is that it is a change in underlying attitudes and levels of understanding that are key to changing the situation for people with disabilities. Indeed it could be argued that if underlying attitudes and levels of understanding were to change in a positive manner then the necessary changes in policy should follow as a natural progression of the new situation. However, writers such as Imrie (1997) and Birkenbach (1990) have argued that perspectives such as the medical and social models are both inherently weak because they deny the interactional character of disablement. Imrie (1997) and Birkenbach (1990) do, however, acknowledge the difficulties of trying to locate disablement in a relationship between a medical and a functional problem and the social responses to it, as they claim the concept of disability requires. Birkenbach (1990) argues that the social model must recognise that there is a physical state that prevents people with disabilities being afforded equal opportunities and treatment in that their very physical differences mean that society has to react to them and their various needs in a different way from the way it reacts to the same needs of the rest of society. French (1993) rejects the idea that her visual impairment generates disabilities that are wholly socially created. As she comments, her impairment (blindness) disables her from recognising people and makes her 'unable to read non-verbal cues or emit them correctly' (French, 1993, p. 17). In response to this Priestley (1998) cites the Northern Officer Group Report of 1996 which states:

> The social model does not deny the existence of impairments and physiological differences ..., rather, it addresses them without attaching value judgements such as 'normality' and shifts emphasis towards those aspects of our world that can be changed.
> (Northern Officer Group (1996) cited in Priestley, 1998, p. 85)

In addition to this Shakespeare and Watson (1997) feel that this issue of the failure of the social model to acknowledge the role of impairments in producing disability is one that only arises within the area of disability research. They feel that the real issue is the need for a clear and united stance, because 'the differences within the movement on the issue of the social model are as nothing compared to the hostility and ignorance with which the social model is greeted in the wider world' (Shakespeare and Watson, 1997, p. 299). Whilst acknowledging the importance of individual impairment in the construction of individual personal identity, Priestley (1998) underlines the importance of the fact that people who are different may still be discriminated against collectively within the society in which they live.

Disability and normality

The concept of 'normality' plays an important role in people's views and perceptions of the world around them and the people in it. Most people's concept of normality is historically and culturally located and so a universal concept of normality would appear impossible, as Morris (1993) points out:

> Prejudice is associated with the recognition of difference. In theory 'normal' could be a value-free word to mean merely that which is common, and to be different from normal would not therefore necessarily provoke prejudice. In practice, the word is inherently tied up with ideas about what is right, what is desirable and what belongs.
>
> (Morris, 1993, p. 101)

Abberley (1993) argues that the range of disciplines, from medical sociology to social psychology, still retain the notion that disabled people are abnormal, in the sense that their impairment can be explained only in terms of a deviation from a 'standard norm' and that they are the problem for deviating from it. Davis (1997, p. 9) discusses the use of 'norms' within society and claims that "we live in a world of norms". He argues that everything we do is compared against that of the 'average person', be it our intelligence, height, weight or sex drive, and that there is probably no area of contemporary life in which some idea of a norm, mean, or average has not been calculated. Davis goes on to argue that in order to understand the disabled body, one must return to the concept of the norm, the normal body. He suggests that the majority of writing about people with disabilities has been centred on the disabled person as the object of study, and argues that a focus on the construction of normalcy would be more advantageous. His argument is that the "problem" is not the person with a disability; the problem is the way that normalcy is constructed to create the "problem" of the disabled person.

Davis' argument that everything we do is ranked along some conceptual line from subnormal to above-average is extended and further related to people with disabilities in the work of Shearer (1981). Shearer discusses the broad mix of abilities and inabilities that goes to make up the human race. She cites the case of a woman who because of an accident of birth, is unable to walk at all and must go about in a wheelchair. The woman is, however, a gifted mathematician and also has a quota of other gifts. However, somehow, according to Shearer, she is no longer seen as able in some situations and un-able in others. Instead, a blanket description is thrown over her. She is 'disabled'. Immediately the perception changes. The continuum of ability and inability is broken and a new vocabulary comes into play. Shearer claims that by turning a description of a condition into a description of people, we are saying that this is all we really need to know about them and in doing so we confirm their 'abnormality'. Barton (1993, p. 44) claims that 'definitions are crucial in that the presuppositions informing them can be the basis for stereotyping and stigmatisation' and by making terms such as 'disabled' a blanket term to cover people with all types of impairment it creates a sense of 'sameness'. This partly explains the strenuous efforts by persons working and competing in the field of disability sport to have those participating described as 'athletes with disabilities' rather than 'disabled athletes' in order to place the emphasis on the fact that, first and foremost, they consider themselves, and would wish to be viewed by others, as athletes (who happen to have an impairment). Moreover, Barton (1993) also claims that the way an individual with a disability experiences their disability within a society and the level of perceived discrimination and oppression can be lessened or compounded by other issues such as race, gender, class and age. This clearly underlines the complexity of how disability is produced and experienced and it is clear from this that simply redefining a few labels will actually do little to change the underlying presuppositions attached to those labels.

Disability and multiple oppression – mediation or magnification

The use of social construction theory, upon which the social model of disability is based, is not confined solely to the field of disability studies. It has been used to investigate many areas of society as the following quote from Figueroa (1993) indicates:

> Racism at the cultural level can be thought of as the operation of a shared racist frame of reference. This is a socially shared set of assumptions, beliefs, conceptual constructs, symbolic systems, values, attitudes and behavioural norms linked implicitly or explicitly to a concept of 'race', ... Thus, this racist frame of reference can be thought of as a group myth, ideology, worldview, shared paradigm or embedded code in which real or supposed phenotypical or other features, taken as natural or inherent defining characteristics, constitute the key differentiating factor. It animates and constrains perception, interpretation and action, defines group identity, provides a rallying point for group loyalty and cohesion, structures social relations, provides a rationale for the existing social order, and performs a system maintenance function, serving the interests of those who hold power. It essentially operates at a tacit or taken-for-granted level.
>
> (Figueroa, 1993, p. 93)

It would appear that the words 'race', 'racist' and 'racism' could quite easily be replaced by words such as class, gender, age, disability, sexual orientation and all of their relevant 'isms' without changing any other words or the overall context and meaning of the quote, although in practice these might be differently experienced. Wendell (1996, p. 37) claims that social factors that have an effect on people's bodies are mediated by other factors such as 'racism, sexism, heterosexism, ageism, and advantages of class background, wealth, and education.' The social construction approach, therefore, allows for the inclusion of numerous possible interrelated factors when investigating each factor's effect (both positive and negative) on individuals or particular social groups. What this also highlights is that an individual can be the victim of multiple prejudices. A black, female, disabled lesbian may be subject to a combination of prejudices such as racism, sexism, disableism and heterosexism, each of which may interact to magnify the sense of isolation within the society in which they happen to live. Alternatively, the impact of some of these 'isms' might be mediated by others so that a white, disabled, heterosexual male from a wealthy background maybe subject to far less prejudice within society, especially if their disability was received as a result of an injury whilst fighting a war for their country.

Disability, language and sport

Language is at its most simple just a series of words or characters. It is the meanings attached by humans to these words or characters that makes language important. One function of language is communication, but in communicating humans also, more often than not, convey the underlying meaning behind the words or characters used. It is also claimed that language plays a key role in politics, domination and control. The meanings attached to the words or characters used are socially constructed within the social or cultural group within which an individual grows up and develops. Therefore, there can be major differences in the perceived meanings of words such as disability, disabled and even what constitutes sport, dependent upon the social and cultural group within which an individual learns their proscribed meanings. However, as some social groups and cultures within a given society are more powerful or have more influence than others one set of meanings for these words may gain dominance, even over those meanings proscribed by the group they refer to. In the next section some of the potential impacts of this power struggle, which is predominantly between powerful groups within the non-disabled majority (such as the medical profession and policy makers and those with economic and political power and influence) and those with the greatest understanding of the impacts of disability and disabling language, people with disabilities themselves, are highlighted.

Ableist language, internalised ableism and feelings of inferiority

Today's mainstream sports organisations, sports media, sports sponsors and the overall sports industry place an extensive focus on non-disabled athletes and non-disabled sports. While sports opportunities for persons with disabilities continue to emerge in many international communities, athletes with disabilities and disability-specific sports largely remain segregated and invisible from the mainstream sports environment. Ableism is defined as discrimination in favour of the non-disabled and against people with disabilities. Historic and current barriers and prejudices have reinforced the marginalisation of persons with disabilities in sports.

In the context of disability sport this prioritisation of non-disabled sport within society devalues sport for athletes with disabilities and potentially undermines much of the hard work done by disability activists to gain acceptance for people with disabilities in all walks of life. Thomas Hehir of the Harvard Graduate School of Education defines ableism as:

> the devaluation of disability ... that results in societal attitudes that uncritically assert that it is better for a child to walk than roll, speak than sign, read print than read Braille, spell independently than use a spell-check, and hang out with non-disabled kids as opposed to other disabled kids.
>
> (Hehir, 2002, p. 2)

Ableism devalues people with disabilities and results in segregation, social isolation and social policies that limit opportunities for full societal participation. Unfortunately, persons with disabilities are also susceptible to internalising stereotypes and negative beliefs. This process is called internalised ableism and is similar to internalised racism and sexism regarding other devalued groups. Internalised ableism in sport is experienced by disabled athletes, coaches and administrators through their acceptance of the status quo and second-class status compared to non-disabled athletes and non-disabled sports.

Disabled athlete – an oxymoron?

So what part does language play in this process? As described earlier, language is made powerful by the meanings ascribed to particular words and phrases and an understanding of those meanings by various groups within society. The non-disabled form is, by far, the largest group within society and also the most powerful, by sheer force of numbers if nothing else. Therefore, non-disabled definitions or meanings for words tend, on the whole, to be the most widely accepted and used. There has, in recent times, with the advent of the social model of disability, been slow but positive change in some quarters regarding the meaning attached to disability. However, for the majority of non-disabled the perceived meaning is still based within the medical model of disability whereby disability has as its emphasis a disability-specific or categorical approach that reinforces and perpetuates the perspective of disability as found in the person and their individual impairment and, therefore, as a problem of the individual. In addition, little headway, if any has been made in altering in any way the meaning attached to words such as 'sport' and 'athlete'. The connection between the human body, physicality and sport is a complex one. However, Barton (1993) claims sport is a social construction of dominant groups within society and is, therefore, a creation of and for the non-disabled, which gives priority to certain types of human movement. According to Middleton (1999) sport is a highly prized activity within society, in which success is well rewarded and applauded. She claims that 'a high value is placed on physical perfection measured in terms of speed, strength, endurance, grace, style and the ability to fight' (Middleton,

1999, p. 65). These highly prized attributes of any top class athlete mean that when words such as disabled and athlete or disability and sport are placed next to each other the general accepted perceptions of each mean that there is an immediate and fundamental contradiction. In an ideal world both words should be simply descriptive nouns to describe a condition and an activity respectively. However, in reality, both are laden with socially constructed meaning and underlying value judgements.

Study activity

Form two groups. One group should argue 'disability sport' is not really sport because ..., whilst the other group should argue that it is, giving their reasons. Afterwards, compare each group's arguments with the three models of disability and see which they fall into and discuss the outcomes.

Conclusion

The apparent oxymoronic nature of terms such as disabled athlete and disability sport are part of the reason why disability sport and disabled athletes find it so hard to be accepted as just sport and just athletes. It further impacts on opportunities for athletes to get involved and advance in disability sport as well as opportunities for the Paralympic Movement to generate media interest and sponsorship deals. Possible reasons for why these issues exist and how they impact upon participation in disability sport are discussed in the following chapters.

Chapter review questions

1   Describe the five phases through which Dunn and Sherrill (1996) argue society has progressed in its treatment of people with disabilities.
2   Outline three key models of disability.
3   Explain the concept of multiple oppression.
4   Why is language important when discussing disability.

Suggested further reading

Barton, L. (ed.), 2006, *Overcoming Disabling Barriers: 18 Years of Disability and Society*, Routledge, London, UK.
Howe, P.D., 2008, *The Cultural Politics of the Paralympic Movement: Through an Anthropological Lens*, Routledge, London, UK.

5 The broader social issues of disability within society and their impact on sports participation

Chapter aims

- Outline the economic and social position of people with disabilities.
- Review the impact of societal perceptions of disability and disability sport upon people with disabilities.
- Introduce some of the barriers to participation in sport for people with disabilities.

The previous chapter outlined some of the ways that societal perceptions of, and attitudes towards, disability might arise and the ways in which these might show themselves. This chapter will now look at some of the more tangible impacts of these perceptions on the daily lives of people with disabilities and upon their opportunities to get involved in sport at all levels.

The economic and social position of people with disabilities

Research worldwide appears to suggest that the economic and social position of people with disabilities is generally quite bad. According to the Spring 2000 Labour Force Survey 7,004,000 of 45,317,000 British residents of working age (16+) are disabled (UK Sport, 2000, p. 6), which equates to around 15.5 per cent of the population who are of working age. According to Southam (1994, p. 13) only 31 per cent of people with disabilities who were of working age were in employment in the mid-1980s and in general these jobs tended to be poorly paid, low status positions (Kew, 1997; Southam, 1994). According to Huang (2005) in Taiwan, a survey in 2004 revealed that 30 per cent of disabled people were unemployed and that the unemployment rate for disabled people was seven times more than the average unemployment rate of the nation (Gao and Liang, 2004 in Huang, 2005). In addition to this Oliver (1996, p. 115) points out that 60 per cent of people with disabilities in both Britain and the USA currently live below the poverty line and as Crawford (1989, p. 8) points out 'for most, the economics of disability determine what life at the sidelines is like'. Oliver (1993a) claims that work is central to industrial societies due to the fact that it not only produces the goods to support life, but also helps to create some of the social relationships necessary for a satisfactory life. Despite these figures, above, French (1994) claims that there is considerable evidence to show that people with disabilities can be just as productive and efficient as their non-disabled counterparts, as well as being far less likely to have accidents at, or be absent from, work. However, she goes on to state that this information is generally not known or ignored and that it is generally presumed that people with disabilities will be unable to cope, may deter or upset clients and are more likely to have accidents.

Oliver (1993a) claims that it has not always been this way. He claims that the arrival of the industrial society, with its regimented production techniques and the speed required to complete set tasks, runs contrary to the kinds of work methods many people with disabilities have been introduced to. His overall argument in this case is that people with disabilities are very likely to suffer exclusion from the work place due to perceived inabilities and, as a result, face a continued creation of dependency upon the state and those around them. This kind of attitude to hiring disabled employees is clearly highlighted by Huang (2005) who claims that the Protection Law for the Disabled in Taiwan, which defines minimum quotas for the hiring of disabled employees in both public and private companies is flouted by many employers. Apparently, 55 per cent of businesses do not hire disabled people, preferring instead to pay the fine of approximately £262 per month for each disabled person they are short of their quota. According to Huang (2005, p. 60) in May 2002, the Taipei City Special Account for Handicapped Welfare had a net balance of US$166 million as a result of these fines. Crawford (2004, p. 12) points out that in Kenya roughly 81 per cent of the parents or guardians of people with disabilities come from groups that subsist well below the poverty line. This, of course, means that for many disabled people around the world just having enough money to feed and clothe themselves is often difficult, let alone having enough time, money and energy to become involved in sport. However, lack of money is not the only reason they may be prevented from taking part as the following sections will show.

The impact of negative perceptions of disability on social interaction in relation to people with disabilities

The persistence of the negative perceptions of disability embedded in the medical model discourse within many societies is based upon a number of factors; for example, the power of the medical profession to define the discourse for disability, the legitimisation of this discourse by other groups and institutions within society, economic arguments, fear of difference and lack of understanding and the use of societal 'norms', combined with a marginalisation by members of society of any person or group that does not conform to those 'norms'. Some, or all, of these factors may interact to inform an individual's perceptions of people with disabilities and, as such, may form the basis for how they act towards a person with a disability and what they might say when discussing people with disabilities. Perhaps this is most clearly illustrated in the actions of people towards an individual, who has for a large number of years been considered a fit, healthy, non-disabled member of society, but due to an accident or disease becomes 'disabled'. Changes in the way people act towards, or interact with, such an individual give a clear indication of a difference in perception of the social status of that individual who has a newly acquired disability. As Hogan (1999) clearly points out:

> Acquired disability signifies a massive change in a person's social position and constitutes a personal crisis for the individual. Identity as a social phenomenon becomes apparent as individuals are perceived by themselves and others as different.
>
> (Hogan, 1999, p. 80)

However, *The Disability Daily* (1998, in Donnellan, 1998) claims that it is a myth that being disabled is easier if you are born that way and so do not know any different, because it is the way that other people react to impairment (and a lack of facilities for disabled people) that makes things difficult for people with disabilities, irrespective of whether their impairments are acquired or congenital. A typical example of this is parents of disabled children who, fearing the child may hurt themselves, keep them away from any form of physical activity that they perceive as dangerous to their health. The suggestion appears to be that physical activity, particularly strenuous physical activity, is not something that people with disabilities are capable of taking part in. Even when they do, it is seen more as a form of physical rehabilitation rather than something done for an ulterior reason or for its own sake. This very same attitude leads many parents to be very reticent to allow their children to take part in potentially beneficial physical activity (both in terms of socialisation as well as physical well-being) for fear that they might get hurt or are incapable of doing the activity (Thierfeld and Gibbons, 1986). This perceived incompatibility between the demands of sport and the capabilities of people with disabilities plays a key role in keeping many people with disabilities of all ages out of sport. In a recent survey of children with disabilities, aged between six and sixteen, Sport England found that 19 per cent of all those surveyed said that they did not take part in any sport due to inhibition or discrimination by the general public (Sport England, 2001, p. 42). In light of this research some of the effects of the perceptions with regard to sport and disability discussed above on the self-perceptions of people with disabilities are highlighted below. By way of a partial explanation of this complex issue Hargreaves (2000, p. 185) states that people with disabilities 'are looked upon, identified, judged and represented primarily through their bodies, which are perceived in popular consciousness to be imperfect, incomplete and inadequate.' As a result of this those closest to someone with a disability, apparently driven by a desire to help them live as 'normal' a life as possible and a misguided perception that they are now somehow incapable of doing anything for themselves, can change the whole nature of a formerly close relationship. Hargreaves (2000) explains this perception of inability, within Western societies at least, in terms of the emphasis placed within these societies upon the desire to achieve 'mastery and perfection' over, and of, nature and our own bodies and how the disabled body is incompatible with this ideal.

However, according to Huang (2005) in Taiwanese society, where 93 per cent of Taiwanese people believe in a mixture of Buddhism, Confucianism, and Taoism, before Western medicine was introduced through missionary activity in the nineteenth century, cultural perceptions of people with impairments were predominantly entrenched in religious discourses. Disabled people were often considered to have received their impairments as a result of some kind of bad deed in a previous life that had offended either a God or a ghost. Although, through the endorsement of Taiwanese Government policy, Western medicine has become the authoritative perspective about the body in contemporary Taiwanese society, making the medical model of disability the dominant ideology, it has not totally displaced the idea of religious retribution (Huang, 2005, p. 109). Crawford (2004, p.13) reports similar issues in Kenya where she cites myths surrounding the passing on of 'bad blood' as one of the perceived reasons for someone having a disability.

The socially constructed 'reality' of disability and sport and some of its effects upon the self-perceptions of people with disabilities

Self-confidence and self-image

When constantly confronted with negative perceptions about their abilities to carry out tasks that most people take for granted, and also bombarded with images of 'physical perfection' that most of the general public could not live up to, it is little wonder that many people with disabilities suffer from low self-esteem (Hargreaves, 2000). Seymour (1989) sums this up when she states:

> the body in which I live is visible to others, it is the object of social attention. I learn about my body from the impressions I see my body make on other people. These interactions with others provide critical visual data for my self-knowledge.
>
> (Seymour, 1989 cited in Hargreaves, 2000, p. 185)

This socially imposed feeling of worthlessness and low self-esteem brought on by the reaction of others to obvious physical difference can have very strong and long-term effects on people with disabilities. This is particularly true for young women who live in societies where physical beauty and attractiveness are revered or as Tiemann (1999) puts it:

> In a society where people are systematically taught to hate and fear old age and disability and equate them with 'ugliness', everybody strives for 'prettiness' and youth. In this society it is especially difficult and stressful for women with physical disabilities to meet these demands. They are perceived in Western-European and North-American society as being inadequate, unable to totally fulfil culturally defined norms and role expectations, especially concerning physical attractiveness, physical activity, motherhood, employment and sexual partnership.
>
> (Tiemann, 1999, pp. 1–2)

In line with this, Hargreaves (2000) claims that the influence of dominant images of gender cause many disabled women to 'choose not to participate in sport because, in common with many able-bodied women, they are influenced more by commodified anti-athletic stereotypes of femininity' (Hargreaves, 2000, pp. 186–7). This perceived fear of failure and low sense of self-worth can act as a strong deterrent, for many people (and especially women) with disabilities, to becoming involved in sport. This is especially true when you consider the fact that placing themselves in a sporting context is very likely to exacerbate the visibility of the very physical differences that lead to these feelings and perceptions in the first place. For a more detailed account of some of the issues encountered by women with disabilities in sport, see Chapter 8.

Dependency

The idea, perpetuated through the perceptions of disability embedded in the medical model discourse, that people with disabilities are incapable of doing things for themselves clashes with the need of human beings to feel a sense of independence within their own lives. Therefore, those individuals with disabilities who do require help to perform certain tasks within their daily lives can be made to feel a burden by the actions (conscious or unconscious) of family, friends and carers. This, combined with the loss of any feeling of independency or control over their lives, can lead many of these individuals to feel that they have become a burden upon society and this feeling is probably compounded by the idea of people with disabilities as non-productive members of society as reported by Middleton (1999) and Priestley (1998). This perception of being a burden and feeling guilt for being unable to do the same things as everyone else are what can cause many people with disabilities to stop asking for help altogether. The fact that people with disabilities do perceive themselves to be a burden may have its origins in the fact that many societies, particularly western industrialised societies, are constructed on the Darwinian premise of 'survival of the fittest' (Barnes, 1994, p. 19), where any request for help or assistance is perceived as a sign of weakness. Any requests for help, or 'acts of charity' as they may be perceived by some, can lead to a major lowering of self-esteem or even depression.

A perceived failure to live up to their role as an independent member of society is often blamed, within the medical model discourse, on the individual's impairment. However, as Morris (1996, p. 10) points out 'impairment does not *necessarily* create dependency and poor quality of life; rather it is lack of control over the physical help needed which takes away people's independence'. Therefore, the combined assumption that the problem lies within the individual and their impairment (Felske, 1994, p. 182) and that everyone, especially adults, should be able to look after themselves and their own needs within a society based upon competition (Middleton, 1999, p. 69) can force people with disabilities into the false belief that they are a burden upon society and that they are to blame for their situation. By leading individuals with disabilities into this kind of self-belief, however, it can help ensure that they do not make too many demands upon society, particularly ones that have economic impacts for society as a whole (Barnes, 1994, pp. 220–1).

Negative perceptions of disability and their influence upon people with disabilities

It could be assumed that negative perceptions with regard to disability are only relevant to non-disabled individuals when dealing with or discussing people with disabilities. However, the power and reach of the perceptions of disability embedded in the medical model discourse are such that they can inform people with disabilities' discourses regarding people with different or more severe impairments in much the same way as they do for the non-disabled community. Just because people with a disability are subjected to one or some of the socially constructed 'isms' (e.g. disablism, sexism, racism) it does not mean that they are immune from using disablist discourse. Indeed, as an example of this Brittain (2004a) quotes one Paralympian as follows:

INA I think it gives a bad impression when you see these people that, like the ones doing boccia. I think that's just such an embarrassment and you know when we went out there and came back then people were saying oh we're not on the same plane as the boccia lot.

INT But those are CPs (cerebral palsied athletes), not intellectually disabled.

INA No, but it's still intellectually or mentally disabled isn't it?

INT They're not, the CPs (cerebral palsied athletes). It's just that they don't have the control of the muscles.

INA Yes, but it's people like that that give the rest of us a bad name and impression and they seem to class us all together and they only see the really bad ones generally.

(Brittain, 2004, p. 443)

It appears then that Ina is displaying a discriminatory or disablist viewpoint of a group of people more severely disabled than herself. Arguably there is a tendency within society to label all people with disabilities as 'disabled' and attribute the same 'meaning' (usually that of the person with the greatest level of impairment) to people with all types of impairment. This then could be why Ina fears being associated with this group. However, in reality the quote from Ina clearly demonstrates a lack of understanding of what it means to have cerebral palsy and also a discriminatory attitude towards their right to be taking part in their chosen sporting activity and being part of the same team as Ina and the others she refers to. In this case, this does not demonstrate the more usual case of non-disabled perceptions regarding disability potentially deterring a potential athlete with a disability from becoming involved in a sport, but another, albeit relatively less, disabled individual displaying the same kind of views about another group of individuals with a disability. This kind of occurrence has also been reported by Hunt (1966 cited in Sherrill, 1986, pp. 23–4) who stated that 'people with less stigmatized disabilities are often quite prejudiced against individuals who are more stigmatized.' This then plays a part in reinforcing and recreating negative perceptions of disability and their continued use within society.

Lack of awareness amongst people with disabilities

Brittain (2002) investigated, as part of a larger research project, how aware the participants in his research were of the impact of societal perceptions of disability on their lives by giving each of the participants taking part in the research three wishes, which they felt, if granted, could improve the situation for disability sport within Britain and/or encourage more people with disabilities to take up sport. Despite the fact that Britain is the birthplace of the social model of disability, not one of the participants directly stated that what was needed was a change in the perceptions of society as a whole towards the issue of disability. Brittain states that although the wording of the question put to them may have been at fault, if the participants in the research were truly cognisant of the mechanisms that result in many of the problems they face, then there would have been a far greater emphasis upon changing 'attitudes' towards disability within society amongst their answers (Brittain, 2002, p. 149). However, this apparent lack of awareness amongst the interviewees is consistent with Lukes's (1974) third dimension of power which is most closely related to the ideas of Gramsci's hegemony theory in which Gramsci (1971) states 'the ascendancy of a class or group rests on its ability to translate its own worldview into a pervasive dominant ethos' (Gramsci 1971 cited in Drake, 1999, p. 14). Drake states that in Lukes' view this involves the shaping of people's perceptions, cognitions and preferences in such a way that they accept their role in the existing order because they can neither see nor imagine an alternative to it. In addition Drake (1999) claims:

there are many examples where disabled people, and more especially carers, unthinkingly accept the medical model and thus strive for individual rather than environmental change.

(Drake, 1999, p. 17)

The above then gives a grounding in some of the issues that disabled individuals have to deal with in their everyday lives and which, when combined together, may have a considerable impact on both their opportunities and desire to become involved in sport.

Sport and disability

Devine (1997) claims that society has a prescribed set of standards by which we are all measured and when someone's biological make-up or function fails to meet these standards they are 'assumed to be inferior and are subject to a decrease in inclusion in society' (Devine, 1997, p. 4). This is equally true for many aspects of life, but in the realm of sport, where one of the key aims is to distinguish between different levels of biological make-up and function through tests of physical strength, speed and endurance, this is especially true. In many ways sport is designed to highlight and revere extremes of bodily physical perfection and, under these circumstances, it is possible to see why, for some people, the idea of elite sport for people with disabilities, and in some cases any sport at all, is an anathema. Mastro *et al.* (1988, p. 81) claim that part of the reason for this is that 'there is no culturally recognised need for competition and sports beyond therapeutic programs', which in itself has its roots in the schism between the socially constructed discourse of what sport is and the perceptions of disability embedded in the medical model discourse. By this I am referring to the view of sport as a means of highlighting bodily perfection and the perceptions embedded in the medical model discourse that views disability as a major form of biological imperfection. The outcome of such a situation for potential athletes with a disability is that their dreams and aspirations can be met with scorn or derision.

Self-perception and sport

Kew (1997) attempts to explain the relatively low number of people with disabilities who take part in sport in terms of a lack of previous opportunity and experience 'at critical learning periods in childhood' (Kew, 1997, p. 112), leading to a low self-assessment of their own abilities. This in turn translates into a fear of failure or ridicule, which causes potential sportsmen and women with disabilities to shy away from or avoid completely any form of sport or leisure activity that may place them in this potential position of perceived failure or ridicule. This appears to support the idea that part of the reason why many people with disabilities do not become involved in sport is based in their own self-perceptions, learnt through numerous interactions with non-disabled members of society and leading to low self-confidence and negative self-images with regard to the capabilities of their own bodies. Indeed, in the Sport England survey of children with disabilities 17 per cent of the respondents cited their own impairment as the major reason preventing them from doing any sport (Sport England, 2001, p. 42).

Material factors

For those people with disabilities who are encouraged to take part in sport or who decide, despite the factors mentioned above, to take part of their own volition the problems that they may encounter along the way are potentially many and varied. The following are just a selection.

Transport

Barnes (1991, p. 186) cites a succession of studies (e.g. Barnes, 1990, GLAD, 1988), which indicate that a major factor in the opportunities for a person with a disability to take part in activities outside their own homes is access to a car belonging to their family or a friend. This dependency upon the goodwill and availability of family and friends for transportation or even on local specialised transport systems has several repercussions for people with disabilities. These include a decrease in independence such that any leisure activities often have to be arranged around those times when transport is available. If transport availability does not happen to coincide with the times when coaching is available, or when team mates train, then the chances of an individual, however keen or talented, achieving their optimal performance level will be severely restricted. Cavet (1998, p. 98) claims that 'there is substantial evidence that disabled young people have more limited opportunities for leisure activities outside their own homes than non-disabled people of the same age'. The GLAD report (1988, p. 3) claims that those people with disabilities who are dependent on specialised transport systems such as local authority provision 'participated in the fewest leisure activities outside the home'. This may, therefore, kill off some elite disability sports careers before they have even begun.

Physical accessibility

Even if problems of time and transport can be overcome, or are not an issue, further problems of accessibility can arise once an athlete with a disability has arrived at their destination. Much has been written about problems of accessibility for people with disabilities (e.g. French and Hainsworth, 2001) and many buildings were designed and built with a conception of non-disabled users in mind. Therefore, if people with disabilities have difficulty entering a facility it may put them off taking part in sport at all. Not only does it make access awkward, but it makes people with disabilities feel unwanted and unwelcome at the venue.

Study activity

Visit your local sports centre. How accessible do you think it is for disabled individuals? Do not just think in terms of wheelchairs. Does the sinage include pictures to assist the intellectually disabled or those who can't read? Do any of the staff have a sign language qualification? Do they offer any activities, integrated or otherwise, for the disabled? If not, try to find out why not.

Time/pace

Just getting dressed or changing can take a lot longer than for non-disabled individuals. Lack of time, the time of day and the time it takes to do things can all play a part in arranging a training regime for a sportsperson with a disability. Wendell (1996, p. 38) claims 'pace is a major aspect of expectations of performance, non-disabled people often take pace so much for granted that they feel and express impatience with the slower pace at which some people with disabilities need to operate'.

Disability specific implications

One example of a disability specific implication is access to guide runners for blind athletes, for both racing and training. Finding and retaining a guide runner for a blind athlete who might be training eight or nine times a week, especially one committed enough and fast enough can be a mammoth time consuming task in itself.

Adapted equipment

The cost and availability of adapted equipment for use by athletes with a disability can have a major impact upon their participation. A single racing prosthetic for a below the knee amputee with fitting costs just under £5,000 (Dyer, 2007, personal communication) and a top of the range Invacare Top End Eliminator OSR Racing Chair costs just under $7,000 (Invacare website, 2007).

Competition at an appropriate level

The relatively low number of people with disabilities taking part in sport, especially competitive sport, can have an impact on opportunities for people with disabilities to get involved and progress within a particular sport. This is further compounded by the athletes having to be split up into functional classification groupings in order to try and ensure fair competition. For a more detailed account of the classification issue, see Chapter 7.

Access to coaching

Just finding a coach willing to take on an athlete with a disability can be a task in itself. Finding one who has the knowledge, or the time and the inclination to gain an understanding, of the implications of a particular impairment on the coaching and training process can prove even harder.

Type of schooling

Brittain (2004b) highlights the impact of schooling on the opportunities for children with disabilities to become involved in sport. In particular he highlights the impact of the move towards mainstreaming of children with disabilities and the implications this has both for children with disabilities and for teachers of physical education within mainstream institutions who are often unequipped to deal with them. This not only has an impact upon participation in disability sport in general, but as Brittain (2004b p. 90) highlights can also have a major impact upon elite level sport, particularly for those impairment groupings such as wheelchair users and visually impaired that are particularly difficult to fully integrate into a mainstream physical education class. In addition, the dispersal of disabled children into mainstream schools has made new talent identification much harder than when they were all together in special schools.

Study activity

Did you have any disabled children in your year at school. If so, what happened to them during games and PE lessons? If they were allowed to take part how easy was it for them to be fully involved and what did the teacher do to try and make this possible?

Overall impact on recruitment of new athletes

The impact of a combination of these factors not only affects recruitment into grass roots disability sport, but also at the very highest levels. According to Brittain (2004b) from 1992 to 2000 only one new visually impaired athlete joined the Great Britain Paralympic track and field squad. In addition, of the nine visually impaired track and field athletes representing Great Britain in Sydney only one was under thirty years of age. The same is also true of the wheelchair team of whom, from the eight athletes present in Sydney, only one was under thirty years of age and she did not compete due to illness. A comparison of the average ages of the five disability groups in the track and field team in Sydney, as well as a comparison of the overall track and field

Table 5.1 A comparison of the average ages of the Great Britain Paralympic track and field team in Sydney by disability grouping and with the able-bodied Olympic track and field team in Sydney

	Men			Women			Team		
	No.	*Age range*	*Ave age*	*No.*	*Age range*	*Ave age*	*No.*	*Age range*	*Ave age*
ALA	4	18–38	27	1	–	26	5	18–38	27
CP	14	17–35	24	7	21–52	28	21	17–53	25
ID	4	19–31	25	0	–	–	4	19–31	25
VI	8	26–40	34	1	–	30	9	26–40	34
W	4	32–49	40	4	21–53	35	8	21–53	38
Team	34	17–49	29	13	21–53	30	47	17–53	29
Olympic Squad	45	21–43	27	30	21–42	28	75	21–43	27

ALA=Amputee and les autres, CP=Cerebral palsy, ID=Intellectual disability, VI=Visual impairment, W= Wheelchair, Team=Whole Great Britain Paralympic Track and Field Squad, Olympic Squad=Able-bodied Track and Field Squad
Source: (Brittain 2004b)

team with that of the British non-disabled Olympic track and field team is given in Table 5.1.

A comparison of the differences in the average ages of the visually impaired (34 years) and wheelchair (38 years) squads with the other disability groupings, where the average age is well below thirty, raises the question of why more young athletes in these two groups are not making it to the top in the sport. Although Brittain accounts for this in terms of the fact that at school the two groups of children with an impairment that are, potentially, the most difficult to integrate into non-disabled physical activity lessons are those with visual impairments and those in wheelchairs, it is likely to be a combination of some or all of the above factors, but especially issues such as accessibility, which have a greater impact for these two impairment groups. Many of the children in the other three disability groupings, although maybe not as quick and mobile as their non-disabled peers, are still able to integrate into a variety of physical activities with minimal or often no adaptations to the activity. These children, therefore, get the maximum number of possible opportunities to undergo the normalisation process and as such gain the maximum potential benefits.

Conclusion

It is clear, then, that the way people with disabilities are viewed by the rest of society can have a great bearing upon both their lives, sporting and non-sporting, and their self-confidence. This issue of self-confidence is particularly true for women with disabilities and is investigated further in Chapter 8. It is also clear that the impacts of these issues are felt all the way from the grass routes introduction to sport for the disabled all the way up to impacting upon the recruitment of new elite athletes with a disability at the Paralympic level.

Chapter review questions

1   How and why does impairment impact upon the economic and social position of people with disabilities?
2   How do non-disabled perceptions of disability and disability sport impact upon how people with disabilities view themselves? What impact might this have on the likelihood of them becoming involved in sport?
3   List some of the barriers people with disabilities might face in getting involved in and progressing within a particular sport.

Suggested further reading

Brittain, I., 2004, Perceptions of Disability and Their Impact Upon Involvement in Sport for People with Disabilities at All Levels, *Journal of Sport and Social Issues*, Vol. 28(4), p. 429–52.

Thomas, N., 2008, *Disability, Sport and Society: An Introduction*, Routledge, London, UK.

6 Media, marketing and disability sport

Chapter aims

- Review the role of the media and the way it represents disability.
- Outline the International Paralympic Committee's response to media coverage of disability sport.
- Outline the costs of running the Paralympic Movement and Games and the increasingly important role of marketing in raising the necessary funds.

The way the media portray people with disabilities and disability sport can have a major impact on how other groups and individuals within society view them also. The combination of how they are portrayed by the media and how the rest of society views them can also have a large bearing upon the success or otherwise of any marketing programmes those running the Paralympic movement might undertake in order to raise the increasing funds necessary to support the significant growth that has occurred in the movement over the last ten to fifteen years.

The media and its representation of disability in general

A lack of understanding towards, and coverage of, disability issues within the media is not limited to just disability sport, but to disability generally. Haralambos and Holborn (2000) point out as a possible reason for this general lack of understanding and awareness that the people who hold senior positions in media organisations are mostly middle-class, and usually older than their subordinates, and in addition to this, people with disabilities are highly under-represented within such organisations. This leads to the situation whereby the dominant groups within (Western) society (usually white, middle class, non-disabled males) hold the key positions within organisations and institutions that are key in influencing the perceptions of those within the rest of society. This can lead to the situation whereby representations of people with disabilities shown on television are all defined by people with little or no knowledge of what it is like to be disabled.

Cumberbatch and Negrine (1992, cited in Haralambos and Holborn, 2000, p. 956) cite ten ways in which people with disabilities are represented on television:

1   Disability or handicap as an emblem of evil.
2   The disabled as monsters.
3   Disability as a loss of one's humanity.
4   Disability as total dependency and lack of self-determination.
5   The image of the disabled as a maladjusted person.
6   Disability with compensation or substitute gift (for example, the blind having compensatory powers).
7   Disability leading to courageousness or achievement.
8   Disability and sexuality: as sexual menace, deviancy, danger stemming from loss of control.
9   Disability as an object of fun or pity.
10 The disabled as an object of charity.

Cumberbatch and Negrine (1992) highlight that people with disabilities are rarely portrayed in a positive or constructive light. They claim that when people with disabilities do appear on screen their role and actions are far more likely to be determined by the nature of their disability and they are far less likely to appear as a person who just happens to have a disability. These portrayals of people with disabilities on television, therefore, continue to reinforce the perception of disability as deficit. The blanket label of 'disabled' is applied and the ability–inability continuum is broken. This is a situation one athlete quoted by Brittain (2002) appears very aware of:

> the physically disabled, there's nothing wrong with our brains, and we've got things that we can do that they probably can't do, you know skills and that kind of thing. But unless they actually see more disabled people being successful at various roles then it's hard to get it across that disabled people are just as able and equal to able-bodied people.
>
> (Ina in Brittain, 2002, pp. 156–7)

Ina's use of the terms 'we' and 'they', meaning people with disabilities and non-disabled individuals, suggests a sense of disenfranchisement from the rest of society and gives an indication of the role that societal perceptions of people with disabilities play in the creation of this by setting people with disabilities up as different or inferior to the rest of society, based upon biology. However, it is not only the type of media representation that affects people's attitudes, but also the amount of coverage disabled people receive. The Broadcasting Standards Commission (1999 cited in Haralambos and Holborn, 2000, p. 956) showed that people with disabilities appeared in 7 per cent of their sample of television programmes and accounted for 0.7 per cent of all those who spoke. Reiser and Mason (1990 cited in Barnes, 1994,

p. 198) suggest that this general absence of people with disabilities from television, coupled with the traditional linking of disability and medicine, reinforces the idea that people with disabilities are incapable of participating fully in everyday life, while at the same time feeding the notion that they should be shut away and segregated.

Media portrayals of disability sport

With limited exceptions, the Paralympic Games is often the only time that disability sport receives any kind of national media coverage in countries around the world. Academic investigation of the media coverage at the Summer Paralympic Games, whilst limited in depth, has been occurring in some form after every Games since Seoul in 1988. These include Seoul (Stein, 1989), Atlanta (Schantz and Gilbert, 2001; Schell and Duncan, 1999), Sydney (Thomas and Smith, 2003) and Athens (Quinn, 2007). Pappous (2008) also did a comparative study of newspaper coverage in five countries of the Sydney and Athens Paralympic Games. Thus far, there appears to have been little or no academic study of media coverage at the Winter Paralympic Games.

A clear indicator of societal attitudes towards disabled and non-disabled sport may be seen in the differences in time spent covering the Olympic and Paralympic Games. Schantz and Gilbert (2001) claim that media coverage of the Paralympics is an indicator of public representations of, and attitudes toward, sport for persons with disabilities. If this claim has any validity it should be evident in the coverage and portrayal of athletes with disabilities, and people with disabilities in general, by the media. It is reasonable to suppose that the relative amount of air time given to the Olympic and Paralympic Games gives some indication as to how these events are differently valued by the programmers. One possible example of this is the amount of airtime that the two Games receive on television. According to Richard (in Brittain, 2002) the difference in airtime given by the BBC to the Sydney Olympic and Paralympic Games is indicative of discrimination against disability sport:

> There was 540 hours available of Olympic showing time on TV and there was ten? Ten or twelve of the Paralympics? That's the sort of discrimination that's going on.
>
> (Richard in Brittain, 2002, p. 152)

Richard is not the only one to hold this kind of view about the discrepancy in coverage given by the BBC to the Sydney Olympic and Paralympic Games. The BBC gave viewers the opportunity on its website, under the heading 'Has the Sydney Paralympics been a success?' to air their views about the BBC coverage of the Sydney Paralympic Games. Typical of the numerous responses they received is the following:

I am so disappointed to find the coverage limited to less than an hour per evening, on at a time when most people are still travelling home from work, and dismissed to BBC2, unlike the Olympics which had a prime time evening slot on BBC1 as well as constant live coverage.

(Carole Neale, England cited on BBC Sport Website)

Media coverage given to an event suggests the 'value' placed on it by programmers. Programmers cover an event for a variety of reasons, be it financial, perceived interest to the viewing public or sponsors or simply newsworthiness. If the BBC provides more airtime to Olympic Sport then it appears that it perceives it to have far greater 'value' than its Paralympic counterpart. Since sport is a creation of and for non-disabled people, which gives priority to certain types of human movement (Barton, 1993) disability sport does not, apparently, provide images that fit within the norms that delineate sporting images within British society. However, this issue is not just restricted to Britain. Huang (2005) reports that in Taiwan there was no live media coverage of the Athens 2004 Paralympic Games and the fact that the Games received any coverage at all was largely due to the fact that the Taiwanese President's wife, who is a wheelchair user, led the Taiwanese team in Athens. A group of nearly forty political journalists followed the President's wife to Athens and reports generally appeared as political rather than sporting news. There was only one professional sports journalist from Taiwan with the delegation. Apparently once the President's wife left Athens, the reporting of the Games all but ceased. Quinn (2007) reports that the Canadian Broadcasting Corporation had around 200 staff in Sydney to cover the Olympic Games. It asked a team of six to stay on in Sydney to cover the Paralympic Games, who produced four one hour shows that were shown in Canada after the Games were over. According to Cashman and Tremblay (2008) TV New Zealand also showed four one hour specials after the Sydney 2000 Paralympic Games had ended and in the United States CBS broadcast a two-hour special entitled 'Role Models for the 21st Century: The Sydney 2000 Paralympic Games' in November, nearly two months after the Games had ended. This practice continued in the United States for both the Athens and Beijing Paralympic Games despite mounting criticism. In response to this there were a number of internet-based petitions protesting at the fact that NBC were going to give blanket coverage of the Olympics from Beijing, but no live coverage of the Paralympic Games.

This worldwide lack of exposure has numerous knock-on effects. It limits the visibility of disability sport, therefore lessening the possibility of non-participating people with disabilities becoming aware of it or inspired to take part themselves. Since young people with disabilities, who are interested in sport, have limited role models with a disability to inspire them they may, therefore, be forced to turn to non-disabled sportspersons as role models. There is a possibility, therefore, that they model themselves and their sporting lives on a non-disabled conception of sport based on (masculine, non-disabled) physical strength and performance. Consequently they may perceive their own performances as inferior. The lack of media coverage is implicated in the lack of recognition of the capabilities of athletes with a disability. In addition, in many countries the interest from the media in disability sport is very fleeting and generally dies away completely within two to three weeks of the Paralympic closing ceremony.

Provision of role models in the printed media

Having visible role models to encourage people into believing they too can possibly take part in sport at a high level plays a vitally important role. The printed media plays a key role in this process through the medium of photographs. However, when it comes to photographs of athletes with disabilities research appears to suggest that there is a distinct lack of visible role models for potential disabled athletes in the print media and especially age or gender specific role models for women and children with disabilities. Hardin *et al.* (2006) examined six copies of four different women's sport, health and fitness magazines over a one year period and examined 6,045 advertising and editorial photographs contained in the twenty four magazines for individuals who had a clearly discernable disability. They found that of 1,437 photographs used in advertising there were zero that contained individuals with a discernable disability and of 4,708 photographs used in editorial content only 13 (0.3 per cent) contained individuals with a discernable disability. With respect to disabled children Hardin *et al.* (2001) carried out the same process on thirty-six issues of Sports Illustrated for Kids over a three year period. They found that of 1,527 photographs used in advertising there were zero that contained individuals with a discernable disability and of 5,565 photographs used in editorial content only 24 (0.4 per cent) contained individuals with a discernable disability. None of the 36 cover pages contained individuals with a discernable disability. This has the effect of not only denying disabled people visible role models, but also reinforces the underlying assumption of the superiority and importance of non-disabled sport within society.

It is not just the news media that are guilty of this process however. Hardin and Hardin (2004) examined fifty-nine general physical education methods textbooks, which would be used in the training of the physical educators and sports coaches of the future and found that no more than six of the textbooks contained photographs of individuals with a discernable disability. They also found that of 2,455 photographs used by the textbooks only 14 (0.6 per cent) contained individuals with a discernable disability. Perhaps more worrying still they found that 10 of these 14 (71 per cent) photographs depicted the disabled person receiving help from a teacher, coach or peer, whereas only 19 out of 2,441 (0.008 per cent) depicted a non-disabled person receiving help. This potentially reinforces the image of disabled people as weak and unable to fend for themselves not just amongst the future coaches and physical educators of the future, but also amongst the disabled population. Brittain (2008) in reviewing many of the key texts currently used at some of Britain's key institutions for the provision of degrees in the area of sports studies, sports management and sports development found that they make little or no mention of disability sport whatsoever. Tomlinson (2007), Jarvie (2006) and Green and Houlihan (2005) all make no mention whatsoever of disability sport. Hylton and Bramham (2008) simply mentions the Disability Rights Commission amongst a list of organisations. Numerous other texts appear to show the same apparent disregard for this growing area of sport.

What's in a picture?

It is not just the lack of photographs in the print media showing individuals with discernable disabilities that has an impact. As hinted above in the work by Hardin and Hardin (2004) the way the photograph is framed and what it depicts can be equally revealing about the underlying attitudes towards disability and disability sport within the mainstream media. Pappous (2008) analysed photographs in two popular mainstream newspapers in Greece, France, Spain, Germany and Great Britain during the periods of the Sydney and Athens Paralympic Games. Firstly he counted the number of photographs used from the Games in each country, which were as shown in Table 6.1

In all cases the number of photographs depicting disabled athletes increased at the Athens Games, which possibly hints at an increasing awareness of the Games amongst the journalists at the newspapers selected. The huge increase in the number of photographs in the Greek papers for the Athens Games also clearly shows the impact and importance of actually hosting the Games. However, on closer examination of the photographs Pappous highlighted a number of issues with the content and framing of the photographs some of which are outlined below:

Hiding the disabled body

Pappous found that in some of the photographs the image had been altered such that the particular impairment of the Paralympian (wheelchair user, amputation, etc.) was not visible. It is as if the editor had decided that these are things that the readers should not be subjected to, thus reinforcing many of the stereotypes regarding disability that are inherent in the medical model.

Table 6.1 Photographs used from Paralympic Games

	France	Germany	Great Britain	Greece	Spain
Sydney 2000	0	14	16	3	4
Athens 2004	4	15	23	105	11

Source: (Pappous, 2008)

The use of passive poses

Many of the photographs used depicted the Paralympians in very passive poses, unlike many of the action shots used to depict non-disabled sportsmen and women. Despite the fact that most of these Paralympians can run, jump, throw, lift, etc., better than most of the non-disabled population their depiction in passive poses simply reinforces the stereotype of disabled people as weak and passive individuals unable to do anything for themselves without assistance.

A focus on the disability

In contrast to the first point of hiding the disabled body Pappous also found that the opposite sometimes occurred when the focus of the photograph was specifically upon the impairment. However, these photographs do not depict the whole individual athlete, but just a part of them such as a prosthetic limb or a wheelchair. Pappous raises the question of what would be the reaction if an Olympic athlete were depicted by a photograph of just a hand holding a racquet or just one of their feet. What this does is to highlight and reinforce a sense of difference between disabled and non-disabled athletes rather than the fact that they are all just sportsmen and women.

Portraying emotion rather than motion

Pappous points out that despite the fact that the motto of the International Paralympic Committee is 'Spirit in Motion', many editors depict the emotion of Paralympic athletes (athletes with tears in their eyes, crying, etc.) rather than strong action shots thus reinforcing the stereotype of disabled people as fragile, delicate and oversensitive.

Overrepresentation of wheelchair athletes

Many journalists, according to Pappous, appear to work on the assumption that disabled equals wheelchair. This stereotype has possibly been reinforced by the facts that the Paralympic Games started as an event for wheelchair users and also that the international symbol for disability is a person in a wheelchair. However, this often leads to the problem that other categories of disability are under-represented in reporting on the Paralympic Games. This is particularly true of many of the more severely disabled athletes. Part of the reason for this and possibly linked to the point regarding the hiding of the disabled body is that the strong muscular upper bodies of wheelchair athletes (when not shown in conjunction with the wheelchair) clearly fit with non-disabled perceptions of what the sporting body should look like.

Language matters

As pointed out in Chapter 4 the language used in describing the achievements, sporting or otherwise, of disabled people is important, because it is often loaded with underlying meaning and perceptions which are often based in the medical model of disability. This is perhaps best portrayed in the work of Thomas and Smith (2003) who analysed British media coverage of the Sydney 2000 Paralympic Games and found that 'Paralympic athletes were on occasions discussed and reported in ways that reaffirmed dominant media portrayals of people with disabilities' (Thomas and Smith, 2003, p. 172). Perhaps the most common occurrence of this kind of medicalised reporting occurs through the use of what is known as the 'super-crip' stereotype.

The super-crip

Hardin and Hardin (2003, p. 249) claim that the use of the 'super-crip' stereotype is often found in the media coverage of disability sport. They claim that the underlying assumption in such depictions is that people with disabilities are 'pitiful and useless until they "overcome" their disabilities through rugged individualism and pull off a feat considered heroic by the mainstream'. This kind of portrayal of disabled athletes places great emphasis on the disability, usually with the intention of evoking an emotional response (such as pity) and thus reflecting and reinforcing the pervasive medicalised perception of disability as personal tragedy without recognising the socio-political dimensions inherent in disability. By taking such an approach the media tend to trivialise the sporting aspect of the disabled individual, with any successes serving merely as the catalyst for a heart-warming 'super-crip' story. Defeats for fancied Olympic athletes or teams are often reported as national catastrophes, whereas defeats for Paralympic athletes are often reported rather patronisingly as valiant efforts by the poor disabled person. It should be pointed out that this situation is improving, albeit slowly, in some countries such as Great Britain, where Paralympic athletes now receive state funding to assist their training leading to far greater expectations in terms of performance. However, despite increasing media coverage of the Paralympic Games, the content of the coverage continues, on the whole, to reinforce medicalised stereotypes of disabled people as 'super-crips' who courageously overcome their disability and the issues that come with it to achieve and to be 'normal'. Darke (1998, p. 187) claims that such portrayals are based in two general themes that are inherent in media portrayals of disability in general. Firstly, the abnormal medical state that disability is considered to be cannot be seen in any way other than as a tragedy. Secondly, the struggle for 'normality', as defined by the non-disabled population, is unquestionably the only thing a disabled individual would desire to achieve owing to the perceived supremacy of the 'normal' body. Huang (2005, p. 205) claims that 'media representations of Paralympic athletes "emotionally experiencing disability" reveal more about what disability means to the able-bodied than the lived feelings and sport experiences and achievements of elite athletes with disabilities.' Huang goes on to claim that as long as athletes with disabilities have got a tragic and charity-based image, their sporting image will continue to be reported in diminished terms by the media, especially in comparison to non-disabled athletes.

The International Paralympic Committee's response to media coverage

Media coverage of the games since the creation of IPC

Growing coverage and increased interest by the media in the Paralympic Games is one indication of a growing interest and awareness of the Games globally. The media has a tendency only to cover news and events that it perceives its audience to have an interest in and so the increasing numbers of accredited journalists at the Games, especially the summer Games, over the last twenty years is testament to that growing interest and awareness. Figure 6.1 shows clearly that the number of accredited media at the Paralympic Summer Games has more than doubled over the last four Games. However, media interest, particularly from the television networks still varies greatly from country to country. In Great Britain the BBC showed nightly highlight programmes from Athens, which attracted up to 2 million viewers. Conversely, in the USA television companies showed very little interest in the Games in Athens and Beijing and viewers in America had to wait for six weeks after the closing ceremony to see a one hour highlights show, despite

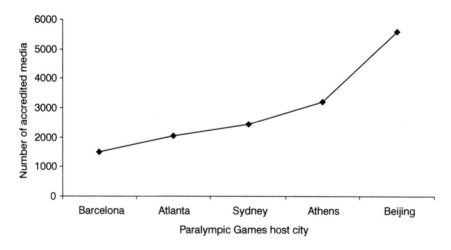

Figure 6.1 Number of Accredited Media at the Paralympic Summer Games (1992–2008)

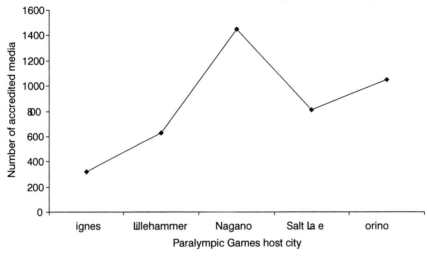

Figure 6.2 Number of Accredited Media at the Paralympic Winter Games (1992–2006)

having one of the largest teams at both Games and an extremely successful record at previous Games.

Figure 6.2 shows a slightly greater increase in media interest in the Paralympic Winter Games compared to that of the Summer Games with nearly four times as many media personnel attending the Turin Games as were in Tignes. However, the overall media presence at the Winter Games is still much lower than that at the Summer Games. The rather prominent peak in attendance in Nagano is likely a reflection of the fact that these were the very first Paralympic Winter Games to occur anywhere outside Europe and so raised greater interest, especially in Asia.

However, overall, the media presence at the Paralympic Games is still nothing like that at the Olympic Games and what coverage there is varies widely from country to country and continent to continent. In order to try and overcome this the International Paralympic Committee launched an internet-based free view television service.

www.ParalympicSport.TV

Although media coverage of the Games is on the increase the disparity between levels of coverage, especially television coverage, led IPC to introduce its own internet-based free view television service that provided a sustainable global media platform with which to reach audiences around the world. Sponsored by VISA and Samsung, this system allows IPC to satisfy additional demand where only limited coverage is available or to provide coverage where none exists. It was first introduced at the Turin 2006 Winter

Paralympic Games and was an instant hit, broadcasting over 150 hours of live sport. The five key objectives of ParalympicSport.TV (PSTV) are:

- To create a sustainable global media platform to reach out to current and potential fans.
- To turn the weakness caused by a lack of mainstream media coverage into a strength as PSTV is often the only coverage available.
- To satisfy additional demand in areas where only limited coverage is available.
- To communicate IPC's vision.
- To make coverage easily accessible in order to allow for maximum exposure.

PSTV has greatly increased awareness of Paralympic sport and by increasing awareness of Paralympic sport it should eventually impact upon traditional media coverage by increasing interest amongst audiences. It has received extremely positive audience feedback and has provided great promotion for the movement. It has also overcome the issue of time difference as spectators are now able to watch their chosen events at a time that suits them from any place in the world. Marketing opportunities and IPC brand communication have also been greatly enhanced, thus greatly improving IPC's long term commercial prospects.

Fans from 110 countries took advantage of this service in Turin, watching an average of just under four and a half hours of sport. In Beijing fans from 166 countries took advantage of the service. It is interesting to note from Table 6.2 (below) that the country that had the greatest percentage of viewers in both Turin and Beijing was the USA, who had been deprived of any live coverage at all of either event by the US networks.

Since Turin, ParalympicSport.TV has been used to provide worldwide coverage of a large number of major sport events for athletes with a

Table 6.2 Percentage audience by nation of the Torino Winter and the Beijing Summer Paralympic Games on ParalympicSport TV

	Torino, 2006		Beijing, 2008	
Rank	Country	%	Country	%
1	United States	21	United States	14
2	Italy	15	Canada	9
3	Canada	11	France	8
4	Germany	8	United Kingdom	8
5	Japan	7	Germany	6
6	France	5	Netherlands	6
7	Netherlands	5	Japan	4
8	United Kingdom	5	Australia	4
9	Begium	4	Spain	3
10	Spain	3	Italy	2

Source: (IPC, 2009; personal communication)

disability including a wide variety of IPC summer and winter sport world championships as well as the annual Paralympic World Cup from Manchester, UK. All of these events are archived on the site and can be viewed again and again, making them an excellent learning resource for anyone wishing to learn more about disability sport.

Study activity

Make a list of as many possible reasons as you can for the differences in the viewing figures on ParalympicSport TV between the Turin 2006 Winter Games and the Beijing 2008 summer games.

The cost of running the paralympic movement and the Games

One of the other key issues, other than general awareness of the Paralympic Games, that media coverage impacts upon is the ability to raise funding and sponsorship. As Table 6.3 (below) clearly shows the costs of putting on both the Summer and Winter Paralympic Games have risen nearly 500 per cent since Seoul, 1988. Obviously these figures reflect the fact that the Games have grown enormously over the last twenty years and, of course, it is the organising committee's job to raise the money to actually stage the Games. However, as pointed out at the end of Chapter 2 the agreement signed between the IPC and IOC in 2003 transferred broadcasting and marketing rights and responsibilities for the 2008, 2010 and 2012 Paralympic Games to the host organising committee in return for fixed sums of money. This means that the ability to raise funding and sponsorship based on the Paralympic brand is not just important for the IPC, but also the host organising committees.

Table 6.3 Summer and Winter Paralympic Games budgets since 1988

Paralympic Games	Games budgets (respective currency)	Games budgets (US$)
Seoul 1988	25 billion Won	32 million US$ (as of 1988)
Tignes 1992	70 million FF	14 million US$ (as of 1992)
Barcelona 1992	9530 million PES	75 million US$ (as of 1992)
Lillehammer 1994	89 million NOK	15 million US$ (as of 1994)
Atlanta 1996	81 million US$	81 million US$ (as of 1996)
Nagano 1998	5510 million Yen	41 million US$ (as of 1998)
Sydney 2000	156 million AUS$	82 million US$ (as of 2000)
Salt Lake 2002	52 million US$	52 million US$ (as of 2002)
Athens 2004	99 million Euro	126 million US$ (as of 2004)
Torino 2006	55 million Euro	69 million US$ (as of 2006)
Beijing 2008	1000 million RMB	150 million US$ (forecast as of April 2007)

Source: (IPC, 2009; personal communication)

IPC also have to raise funds for their own administrative and other running costs. Table 6.4 (below) shows the overall IPC revenue and expenditure for the four year period 2004 to 2007. As can be seen IPC actually ran at a net loss in 2004. This is possibly because this was a Paralympic Games year, which will incur extra costs in relation to the build up and preparation with site visits, etc. Since 2004 IPC has managed a relatively small surplus each year. Unfortunately, the budget for 2008 is not yet available and so it is not clear what impact the $9million the Beijing organisers were due to pay IPC will have on IPC finances.

What is clear from Table 6.5 is the increasing role and importance that income from marketing, sponsorship and fundraising has had on the financial fortunes of the IPC. Income from these sources nearly trebled over the four year period. The overall impact of income from marketing, sponsorship and fundraising rose dramatically over the period. In 2004 it only made up 26.6 per cent of all income for the year. By 2007 it had a risen to 72.9 per cent of all income for the year. This clearly indicates an increasing success on behalf of IPC over the period to market the Paralympic brand as a fundraising tool for the movement and the next section will look at some of the ways they went about it and the issues they had to overcome. What will be interesting to note over the next year or so will be the impact of the global economic downturn on IPC's financial fortunes, especially as they appear to have become so dependent financially on marketing, sponsorship and fundraising as a source of income.

Table 6.4 IPC overall income and expenditure for 2004–2007

Year	Revenue (€)	Expenditure (€)	Result (€)
2004	4,677,507	5,608,496	–390,389
2005	3,409,611	3,325,019	+ 84,592
2006	5,186,401	5,131,156	+ 55,245
2007	4,334,980	4,272,488	+ 62,492

Source: (IPC Website, 2009a)

Table 6.5 IPC income and expenditure from marketing, sponsoring and fundraising activities for 2003–2007

Year	Income (€)	Expenditure (€)	Result (€)
2004	1,244,450	94,676	+ 1,149,774
2005	1,998,191	163,172	+ 1,835,019
2006	2,214,956	122,510	+ 2,092,446
2007	3,161,663	138,767	+ 3,022,896

Source: (IPC Website, 2009b)

Marketing the paralympic brand

According to Hardin and Hardin (2003, p. 246) 'the biggest difference between the Olympic and Paralympic Games lies in awareness and publicity for the events'. Huang (2005, p. 206) takes this further when she states 'Paralympic sport is yet to be regarded as competitive and as valuable as Olympic sport and in consequence the achievements and physical prowess of elite athletes with disabilities are still far from being fully recognised'. In many ways the Paralympic Movement has adopted many of the strategies used by the IOC in trying to market itself to the world. Obviously, however, it does not have the same history or totally the same vision as the IOC. Therefore, in order to provide a strong and viable platform from which to market itself to the world, IPC, as part of its strategic review, came up with a vision for the Paralympic Movement that they felt would get across best the aims and objectives of the Paralympic Movement to sponsors and spectators alike:

The IPC Vision

> To enable paralympic athletes to achieve sporting excellence and inspire and excite the world

Each word in the vision has a clear meaning in defining the ultimate aim of IPC:

1 To *enable*: the primary role of IPC as an organisation: To create the conditions of athlete empowerment through self-determination.
2 *Paralympic athletes*: the primary focus of IPC's activities, in the context of Paralympic athletes, is the development of all athletes from initiation to elite level.
3 To *achieve sporting excellence*: the goal of a sports centred organisation.
4 To *inspire and excite the world*: the external result is our contribution to a better world for all people with a disability. To achieve this, relations with external organisations and the promotion of the Paralympic Movement as a whole are of prime importance.

(IPC Website, 2009c)

According to Schäfer (2008, personal communication) 'in order to achieve the IPC vision, the IPC strategic plan has identified five strategic goals of which one is global recognition. The IPC Strategic Plan (2006) claims that global recognition will be achieved by having a Paralympic brand that is clearly defined and recognised, understood and valued around the world. The overall proposed outcome of this is that IPC should end up with a brand that has clearly defined attributes and messages and that is recognised in the sporting arena, instantly understood by the spectators and the media and valued by its commercial and other partners. In order to achieve this, the strategic plan outlines six strategies:

1   To define and protect the Paralympic brand, including values, key messages and key distinctive characteristics, and to increase the control of the worldwide usage of IPCs marks and properties.
2   To develop and implement marketing and communication strategies that maximise the recognition, understanding and exposure of the Paralympic brand.
3   To determine and implement a sponsorship and fundraising strategy in alignment with the positioning of the Paralympic brand in the market place.
4   To establish the Paralympic brand as a credible vehicle to reach, access and capture the market of persons with a disability and their allies.
5   To ensure the capturing, cataloguing, conservation and access to the history and legacy of the Paralympic Movement.
6   To develop and realise a global education initiative directed to build the awareness and understanding of the Paralympic values among youth and schoolchildren.

(IPC Strategic Plan, 2006, p. 9)

Plate 6.1 Paralympic Mascots have become a major part of the marketing of the Paralympic Games since their inception in Arnhem, 1980 and are always a big hit with the spectators

Some of the ways IPC have attempted to achieve these strategies, other than through the Paralympic Games and other international disability sports events include the following:

IPC Website

Like nearly all major organisations IPC has its own website that enables it to disseminate all the latest news and to provide a range of services to a variety of interested parties from athletes to the media to school children doing projects. It can be found at www.paralympic.org.

The Paralympian

A quarterly newsletter available electronically from the website or in hard copy by registering your details online.

Paralympic school days

This is a set of activities that educate young people about Paralympic sport, individual differences and disability issues in a fun and playful environment. These activities can be organised during a normal school day and target an audience of young students between the ages of 6 to 15. A manual, activity cards and DVD are available to teachers for download from the IPC website.

Paralympic Games Education Programme:

IPC works closely with Paralympic Games Organising Committees to assist them in creating and delivering an education programme leading up to and during the Paralympic Games that will be distributed to schools in that country. For the next Games in Vancouver 2010 a fully web-based Education Programme is being developed for the Olympic and Paralympic Games, targeting students, teachers and the broader public with the aim to educate about the Olympic and Paralympic Movements, sport and culture. It can be found at www.vancouver2010.com/en/edu.

ParalympicSport TV

As described earlier, this has been developed by IPC to try and overcome the major global disparities in media coverage of Paralympic sport and has enabled IPC to overcome other issues such as time changes, whilst giving them full editorial control over how Paralympic sport is portrayed to the world.

IPC YouTube Channel

IPC uses its YouTube channel to broadcast 'SIXTY Seconds' the ParalympicSport.TV news format during Games time. It shows the best scenes of the day presented by IPC Ambassador and former Paralympian Chris Waddell. During the Beijing Paralympic Games the IPC YouTube video clips captured more than 1.2 million views.

Paralympian ambassadors

In February 2008, IPC launched the Paralympian Ambassadors Programme. The aim of this programme is to create a group of top past and present Paralympic athletes to act as ambassadors of the Paralympic Movement, in order to be role models for young people with and without disability and act as awareness and communication tools for the Paralympic Movement to enhance and increase its public profile. There are currently eleven ambassadors worldwide:

Verena Bentele (GER)	Cross country skiing and biathlon
Hou Bin (CHN)	Athletics (High jump)
Cheri Blauwet (USA)	Athletics (Wheelchair racing)
Kirsten Bruhn (GER)	Swimming
Muffi Davis (USA)	Alpine skiing
Dame Tanni Grey-Thompson (GBR)	Athletics (Wheelchair racing)
Michael Teuber (GER)	Cycling
Ernst van Dyk (RSA)	Athletics (Wheelchair racing)
Esther Vergeer (NED)	Wheelchair tennis
Chris Waddell (USA)	Alpine skiing and athletics
Henry Wanyoike (KEN)	Athletics (long distance running)

(IPC Website, 2009d)

IPC Honorary Board

The main purpose of the IPC Honorary Board is to allow leaders of society an opportunity to support the vision of the Paralympic Movement and to strive to maintain the issue of sport for persons with a disability high on the agenda of the global community. Honorary Board Members assist the IPC in creating opportunities for raising awareness and funding, through the members' network of contacts and sphere of influence. There are currently nine members of the IPC Honorary Board:

- HRH Princess Margriet of the Netherlands (NED)
- HRH Grand Duchess Maria Teresa of Luxembourg (LUX)
- HRH Crown Princess Victoria of Sweden (SWE)
- HSH Prince Albert of Monaco (MON)
- Dr James Wolfensohn (AUS) (Former President of the World Bank)
- Ms. Maria Guleghina (RUS) (Opera singer)
- HRH Princess Haya Bint Al Hussein (JOR)
- Ms Thérèse Rein (AUS) (Wife of Australia's Prime Minister Kevin Rudd)
- Mr Hassan Ali Bin Ali (QAT) (Chairperson – Shafallah Centre for Children with Special Needs)

(IPC Website, 2009e)

Study activity

Design further strategies that IPC might use to strengthen further and spread its vision to as wide an audience as possible in a positive way.

Conclusion

It is clear that the amount of media coverage and the way that coverage is displayed can have a major impact upon all areas of disability sport ranging from the recruitment of new athletes to the ability of IPC to raise funding through commercial sponsorship and marketing opportunities. It appears that, on the one hand, IPC is doing everything it can to project a strong and dynamic vision and image for the movement and on the other, changes in the way disability sport is viewed within both society in general and the media in particular are having a positive impact upon the ability of IPC to raise funding through marketing, sponsorship and fundraising opportunities. However, on a note of caution the apparent increasing reliance by IPC on this source of funding shown in Tables 6.4 and 6.5, especially in the current economic climate, may be problematic for the future, although the guaranteed income from broadcasting and marketing rights for the Games of 2008 onwards may go some way to alleviate this.

Chapter review questions

1 List the ten ways Cumberbach and Negrine (1992) claimed people with disabilities have been represented on television and try to explain the implications of some of these depictions for people with disabilities.
2 Describe some of the ways photographs of athletes with a disability are manipulated by the media and the possible reasons why this happens.
3 Describe the concept of the 'super-crip' and explain the implications.

Suggested further reading

Disability Now and National Union of Journalists, Undated Pamphlet, Hacked Off: A Journalist's Guide to Disability (www.nuj.org.uk/getfile.php?id=244) accessed 27-11-08.

Pointon, A. (ed.) with Davies, C., 1997, *Framed: Interrogating Disability in the Media*, British Film Institute, London, UK.

7   Major issues within the Paralympic Movement

Chapter aims

Highlight some of the major issues within the Paralympic Movement:

Cultural or sports games?
Olympians or Paralympians?
Classification
Cheating

Like nearly all major international organisations, sporting or otherwise, the Paralympic Movement has a number of ongoing issues that it has to deal with and mediate. As is usually the nature of such issues they are both complex and difficult to manage in a way that keeps everyone happy. Other issues such as cheating, in various forms, is possibly a reflection of the increasing importance of the Games themselves and the vastly improved benefits that being successful at the Paralympic Games may now bring to both individuals and the nations and sporting organisations that they represent. The aim of this chapter is to outline some of these issues for the reader, although given the complexity of some of them and the limited space available here they can only be presented in their broadest form. Hopefully, however, the reader will be inspired to learn more about the complex nature of these issues and their impacts.

The Paralympic Games – a cultural or a sports event?

The Paralympic Movement and its underlying language/message

From its inception in the late 1940s the founder of the international disability sport movement, Ludwig Guttmann, described the aims of his use of sport in the rehabilitation process of the spinally injured to be social re-integration and to change the perceptions of the non-disabled within society regarding what people with disabilities were capable of (see Chapter 1). This continued to be the underlying message of the International Paralympic Committee

(IPC) regarding the Paralympic Games and international disability sport for many years. These kinds of aims and the language associated with them (e.g. social integration, changing perceptions, etc.) possibly led to the Paralympic Games being perceived primarily as a cultural games rather than one that is about sport. Cultural games have as their aim an ethos of fostering self-respect and belief amongst their participants as well as helping to solidify their social identity as a group. Other examples of cultural games include the Gay Games and the Maccabiah Jewish Games. However, the last five years or so, have seen a distinct shift in the language used and the aims set out by the International Paralympic Committee. The language used is now much more about sport than disability as the very first item on the mission statement of IPC clearly shows:

> To promote and contribute to the development of sport opportunities and competitions, from initiation to elite level, for Paralympic athletes as the foundation of elite Paralympic sport ... To promote the self-governance of each Paralympic sport either as an integral part of the international sport movement for able-bodied athletes, or as an independent sport organization, whilst at all times safeguarding and preserving its own identity.
>
> (IPC Website, 2009c)

Although references to identity and integration are still inherent within the statement the focus is explicitly on sport and sporting opportunities. There is no mention of disability with the exception of its inherent connection with the word Paralympic and all the mentions of the word Paralympic are in connection with elite athletes and sport. It is possible that the reasons for this change hinge upon the fact that the advent of the social model of disability and the increasing influence of disability politics within societies in general meant that recognition of disability issues was much more prevalent. This allowed disability sport and elite disability sport in particular to shift the focus of its aims away from the acceptance of people with disabilities as potentially productive members of society to gaining their acceptance as elite athletes irrespective of any impairment they might have. So why is this important? Perhaps this is best shown by looking at the potential outcomes of the cultural and sporting models in terms of their aims and the language used.

The impact of the cultural and sport models on the Paralympic Movement's place in international sport

There can be little doubt that, historically speaking, there was a definite need for the disability movement in general to take a cultural model approach in all areas in order to try and remove the cloak of near invisibility cast over it by the rest of society and to highlight the fact that people with disabilities were capable of amazing feats, just like anyone else within society. One of the most successful and visible avenues through which these aims have been achieved is through sport. However, disability sport has been so successful that the language and aims of the cultural model approach reached a point whereby they were preventing people with disabilities from being accepted in some quarters as athletes within non-disabled definitions of what constitutes an 'athlete'. As pointed out in Chapter 4, this often conjures up images of physical perfection and sporting prowess that most of the non-disabled population could never achieve. By constantly referring to disability and the exploits of 'disabled' sportsmen and women this not only re-emphasised an element of difference, but also continued to highlight the oxymoronic nature between the non-disabled understandings of words such as 'disabled' and 'athlete' when the two words were brought together. By taking a sports model approach, which emphasises the athleticism of athletes with disabilities and using words such as Paralympian, which, although still understood to mean an athlete with disability, negates the need for any mention of the disability itself, the aims of the cultural model approach can still be achieved without the inherent problems of such an approach as mentioned above. By becoming 'Parallel Olympians' athletes with disabilities can try to get away from the oxymoron that 'disabled athlete' may be perceived as and associate themselves with a movement that sells itself as being about sport as a vehicle for peace and understanding as well as sport of the very highest level. In this way both the cultural and sporting aims of the Paralympic Movement can be met in a positive and constructive context. However, a number of Paralympians refer to themselves simply as Olympians. In the next section, therefore, some of the possible implications of this are investigated. If elite athletes with disabilities were to become fully integrated into the Olympic Movement, although not necessarily in the one Games scenario, would this be a positive step forward for the Paralympic Movement or would this lead to the issue of disability becoming invisible again under a cloak of 'Olympism' and the cultural model impacts of the Paralympic Movement being lost altogether?

Elite athletes with disabilities – Olympians or Paralympians?

Historical context

Before discussing the possible implications of full integration of Paralympic athletes into the Olympic Movement it is worth pausing to look briefly at the historical background with regards to the integration process that has occurred thus far. As early as 1949 Dr Guttmann gave a speech in which he made the claim that the Stoke Mandeville Games would one day become recognised as the paraplegic's equivalent of the Olympic Games. Throughout his career Guttmann consistently drew parallels between the two movements as highlighted in Chapter 2. In the 1970s and 1980s the

Paralympic Movement even went as far as using Olympic terminology such as 'Olympics for the Disabled' to denote the Games that occurred in the Olympic year, which led to threats of litigation from the IOC. In 1984 the IOC consented to demonstration events without any medal status being held at the Sarajevo Winter Games and the Los Angeles Summer Games. At that time the Paralympic Movement, however, saw this as just the first step and in the early 1990s the International Paralympic Committee set up a Commission for the Integration of Athletes with Disablities, which lobbied for, amongst other things, the inclusion of events with full medal status within the Olympic Programme. This was never achieved and although the two wheelchair demonstration events continued to be held at the Summer Olympic Games up until Athens, 2004 the competitors did not receive full Olympic athlete status accreditations. They were not allowed to march in the opening or closing ceremonies nor were they allowed to stay in the Olympic Village.

The rights of athletes with disabilities versus the potential impacts

The modern day usage of the term Paralympic is now widely accepted as being a shortened version of the term Parallel Olympics. However, additional definitions of the prefix 'para' are of interest due to their potentially negative connotation:

> Para-
> Etymology: Greek, from *para;* akin to Greek *pro* before
> 1a : beside : alongside of : <*par*enteral>
> 1b: Parallel
> 1d: associated in a subsidiary or accessory capacity <*para*military>
> 4a : faulty : abnormal <*par*esthesia>
> (Webster's Third New International Dictionary, 1961, p. 1634)

It is the third and fourth definitions that are of particular concern as 'para' can infer that the Paralympic Games are 'faulty', 'abnormal', 'associated in a subsidiary or accessory capacity' to the Olympic Movement. Although the first two definitions indicate the two Movements are parallel to one another, the other definitions have the potential to disempower elite athletes with disabilities. Is 'Paralympian' an appropriate label to use, therefore, if it can be associated with negative connotations? Another reading of the prefix 'para' in Paralympian, in which parallel may be interpreted as disempowering, results from the insinuation that the Paralympic Movement takes a subsidiary capacity to the Olympic Movement. Aimée Mullins of the USA, a multi-Paralympic medallist had this to say on the matter:

> There is indeed a 'less than' association with the Paralympics. It's why I always say that I'm an Olympian and dare anyone implicitly to say

that I'm not, because to do so would only be to 'qualify' my athletic achievements rather than acknowledge them in the same pantheon as that of an Olympic achievement.

(Mullins in Brittain and Wolff, 2007)

The push for full integration by the International Paralympic Committee that was so prevalent in the early 1990s has been replaced by attempts to build up a strong Paralympic brand image, the use of much more sports based language in order to try and gain acceptance of athletes with disabilities as athletes and a gradual move towards a greater use of educational tools such as the International Paralympic day. However, there are those that would argue that sport for the disabled has accepted its status as separate and unequal instead of continuing to advocate for full inclusion in the Olympic Movement due to insecurity and internalised inferiority. Conversely, there is also an argument to be made that the need by athletes with disabilities to call themselves Olympians is also a result of this internalised inferiority in that they are trying to take on the sporting terminology of the non-disabled majority in order to gain acceptance rather than making the term Paralympian one they and others can be proud of in that it encapsulates both their sporting and cultural identity.

Study activity

Make a case with supporting arguments, either for or against athletes with disabilities being fully integrated into the Olympic Movement and then list what the positive and negative impacts of your decision might be on the Paralympic Movement and athletes with disabilities.

The recognition of cultural identity has always been a major part of the elite sporting model. You only have to look at examples such as Cathy Freeman and her attempts to increase the visibility of her aboriginal heritage, the 'black power' salute at the 1968 Men's Olympic 200m medal ceremony or the protests by Islamic Fundamentalist Groups against the clothing worn by Hassiba Boulmerka of Algeria in winning World and Olympic track titles that went totally against what her culture and religion dictated were right and proper. But these are all political issues you might claim. However, to most people the right to promote and defend their cultural heritage is a political issue and this is why the cultural identity model element of the Paralympic Games has been so important to athletes with disabilities in furthering the cause of all people with disabilities. However, amongst the athletes in particular and the Paralympic Movement in general there is a strong move to have athletes with disabilities accepted as athletes first and foremost, whilst still maintaining other elements of their cultural heritage such as race, gender or disability. This is perhaps best summed up by Sarah Reinertsen, a triathlete who has worn a prosthetic leg since the age of seven:

I've always been fighting to be seen as an athlete, but also as a disabled woman. For so long I wasn't included in sports, so I feel every person, regardless of gender or disability, has a right to be an athlete.

(Reinartsen in Brittain and Wolff, 2007)

The argument most often used against integration is that athletes with disabilities would once again become invisible. However, Terri Lakowski at the Women's Sports Foundation claims this is a myth and that until there is integration athletes with disabilities will always feel that they are second-tier (Lakowski in Brittain and Wolff, 2007). There can be little doubt that many of the reasons for these apparent feelings of perceived inferiority are based in the meanings attached to the language and terminology that surrounds sport. There still remains a great need for many of these perceived meanings to be challenged and re-defined. Sport for people with a disability is a highly legitimate category of sport and if Olympism really is about peace and mutual understanding amongst different cultures, rather than money and political power, as it is often perceived to be, then disability sport has a major role to play in that process within the Olympic family. Whether this is best served by full integration of disabled athletes into Olympic and other non-disabled sporting terminology or whether they continue down the 'Parallel Olympic' route is still open to debate and requires more research and thought. However, what does appear to be clear is the importance of the cultural identity element of disability sport as a tool for changing the understanding of perceived meanings. If full integration is to be pursued then a way must be found to ensure that this cultural identity element remains strong and highly visible. An excellent recent example of this is the introduction of a new law drafted in Russia's State Duma on 28 October 2008 that assured the status of the Olympic and Paralympic Winter Games and announced the introduction of IOC and IPC standards to Russia's national legal system. This new law, introduced in light of their successful bid for the Olympic and Paralympic Winter Games in Sochi in 2014 is expected to increase greatly the awareness of disability sport within Russia and it is hoped that it will greatly benefit the 11 million Russians living with a disability (IPC Website, 2009f).

Classification in Paralympic sport

This is possibly one of the most contentious issues in disability sport and also one of the most difficult to find a solution to that satisfies the needs and desires of all concerned. Different impairments impact upon an individual's functional ability in different ways and to different degrees, but in nearly all cases the impacts usually lead to a competitive disadvantage in sport. This is especially true when compared to non-disabled sportsmen and women, but may also be true in comparison to athletes with different impairments or even athletes with the same or a similar impairment. It is necessary, therefore, to put criteria in place in order that success is determined by 'skill, fitness, power, endurance, tactical ability and mental focus' (BOCOG, 2008) as it is in non-disabled sport, rather than by level of disability. A very crude analogy would be to compare classification in disability sport to weight categories in boxing, but the criteria used in classification for disability sport are much more detailed and require much more than just a set of weighing scales. The classification system in disability sport in general and in the individual sports that athletes with disabilities take part in are constantly evolving as classifiers and those involved in running disability sport learn more about the impacts of various impairments on sporting ability. In general classification decides two main issues:

1   Which impairment groups can compete in a particular sport i.e. in goalball only individuals with a visual impairment can compete, but swimming is open to all impairment groups?
2   Which individual athletes, with which impairments and at what levels of impairment, may compete against each other in a particular medal event?

The decision as to which events and who a particular athlete with a disability should compete against is made by a panel of classifiers. The role of a classifier, who usually will only classify athletes within one particular sport that is their area of expertise, is to decide, based on a number of factors, a sports classification grouping for each individual athlete to take part in in their sport. These factors may include the results of a physical examination, a series of practical sports specific tests and even watching individuals perform within a competitive sports setting. Each individual is then assigned a sports classification for that particular sport. Who each individual athlete then competes against will be down to the type of classification system used within a particular sport. Within the Paralympic Movement there are currently two different types of classification system in use:

1   A general glassification system: this kind of classification system only takes into account the type and degree of impairment associated with each individual athlete e.g. the level of visual impairment. Athletes with similar impairments and levels of impairment then compete against each other.
2   A sport specific or functional classification system: in this system athletes are evaluated in terms of their functional ability to carry out specific tasks required by a particular sport e.g. the level of ability to catch or throw in wheelchair rugby.

In general, functional classification systems are associated with physical impairments and general classification systems are usually applied to visually impaired or intellectually disabled athletes. In Paralympic terms the only sports in which visually impaired athletes compete alongside their physically disabled counterparts are in the sports of equestrianism, sailing and Nordic

Plate 7.1 Swimming uses a functional classification system for all physically disabled swimmers

skiing. Some sports such as athletics and swimming may actually employ both systems i.e. they use a general classification system for the visually impaired participants (and the intellectually disabled participants when allowed to compete) and some events for physically disabled athletes and a functional classification system for the remaining participants in certain events (i.e. some field events in athletics and all individual swimming events for physically disabled swimmers). Pickering Francis (2005) claims that the need for the Paralympic Movement to provide categories for athletes that are both entertaining for spectators and fair for the athletes involved requires 'striking a very difficult balance between categories that are sufficiently broad to provide compelling competition yet sufficiently well defined so that people with relevantly similar skills are paired against each other' (Pickering Francis, 2005, p. 129).

Classification and the inherent tensions in the cultural-sporting model dichotomy

Classification is one area of the Paralympic Games where the inherent tensions in the cultural model-sports model dichotomy become very clear. As IPC has moved the Paralympic Games further towards the sporting model the pressure to provide an event that is saleable to sponsors and the media has increased or as Howe and Jones (2006) put it:

> The only evaluative criteria relevant to such logic are supply, demand and profit. Good Games are profitable ones, good sports are marketable ones, and good athletes are endorsable ones. The IPC are conspiring with the IOC to repackage, remarket, refresh, modernize, and essentially sell the Paralympics. The product, however, needs revising to increase demand. The Paralympics needs to be quicker, slicker, shorter, with fewer events and fewer, but higher profile champions.
>
> (Howe and Jones, 2006, p. 33)

As will be seen in the next chapter there has been a squeeze on athlete numbers and a propensity towards reducing the number of medal events at the Paralympic Games since they first returned to the Olympic host venues in Seoul, 1988. However, this move towards achieving the goals laid out by Howe and Jones above comes at a price. Women and athletes with high support needs have been particularly hard hit as will be shown further in Chapter 8. This means that although IPC might be successfully moving towards an elite sports model for the movement the further they move away from the cultural model the more in danger they become of isolating key groups of the community of athletes they are there to represent. This happens because either there are insufficient athletes from a range of countries and continents to make up what the organisers deem a competitively viable event or alternatively these athletes are combined with another classification group that they deem themselves not able to compete against on equal terms and so decide to either change events or sports or sometimes to give up sport altogether.

Another problem that makes the issue of classification even harder to solve to the satisfaction of all concerned is the difficulty of designing a system within a particular sport that is easy for non-disabled spectators to understand. In general, spectators, particularly non-disabled spectators, lack an understanding of disability in general and specific impairments in particular on sporting performance. Combine this with a general lack of anatomical and physiological understanding of the body and how it works and it is easy to see why many people find classification a confusing concept. Unfortunately, as Howe (2008) points out, even though media coverage of disability sport has increased greatly over the last twenty years there is often little or no mention of classification within this coverage even though an awareness, and some understanding, of the classification process would greatly assist in the public's perception of sport for the disabled. Without this understanding and with only non-disabled sport as a benchmark against which to measure any sport for the disabled these spectators might watch, it is likely that their perceptions will remained grounded firmly in the medical model of disability.

Cheating in Paralympic Sport

Many people find it hard to believe that cheating occurs in sport for the disabled. This possibly reflects a perception of sport for the disabled that is grounded more in pity for these poor unfortunate individuals than one that views them as athletes who simply happen to have an impairment. The growing media coverage and increasing rewards now available to individuals who are successful at the highest levels of disability sport and the increasing importance placed on being successful at the Paralympic Games by national governments mean that the pressure to succeed leads to a win at all costs mentality amongst some individuals. Many of the forms of cheating that have long been known about in international non-disabled sport are now also prevalent in elite sport for the disabled. Although cheating is to be deplored in any sport, disabled or non-disabled, what it does highlight is that athletes with disabilities are as human as everyone else with the same wants, desires and potential character flaws that lead them to cheat.

Doping

Much has been written about the illegal use of drugs for performance enhancement purposes within non-disabled sport. Drugs cheats also occur in disability sport. However, the problem is made far more difficult in disability sport by the fact that some athletes actually need to take drugs on a regular basis for health reasons.

Dope testing at the Summer Paralympic Games appears to have begun at the Stoke Mandeville Games in 1984 when eight urine samples all tested negative. Since then the number of tests taken at each Games has increased dramatically with over a thousand tests being carried out in Beijing, 2008. Dope testing at the Winter Paralympic Games began in Tignes, 1992 and despite a steadily increasing number of tests at subsequent Games the first and only case of a positive test at a Winter Paralympic Games occurred in Salt Lake in 2002 when German Nordic skier Thomas Oelsner tested positive after winning two gold medals in men's standing biathlon events

Table 7.1 Doping tests at recent Summer and Winter Olympic and Paralympic Games

	Olympic Games		Paralympic Games	
	Tests	*Positives*	*Tests*	*Positives*
Barcelona, 1992	1873	5	300	3
Lillehammer, 1994	529	0	49	0
Atlanta, 1996	2000	6	450	0
Nagano, 1998	621	1	52	0
Sydney, 2000	2100	11	630	11
Salt Lake, 2002	825	7	97	1
Athens, 2004	2815	17	735	10
Torino, 2006	1219	1	242	0
Beijing, 2008	4900	9	1155	3

(*The Paralympian*, 2002, p.2). As can be seen in Table 7.1 there has only been one Summer Paralympic Games (Atlanta, 1996) where no positive tests have been returned during the Games since 1992. The other four Summer Games have returned a total of 27 positive tests. In the same period there have been 48 positive tests at Olympic Summer Games. Perhaps a little surprisingly this means that the Summer Paralympic Games have returned one positive test for every 121 tests carried out, whereas the rate for the Summer Olympic Games is one positive test for every 285 tests carried out. However it should be pointed out that the vast majority of these positive tests (70 per cent) have all occurred in one sport – powerlifting. Introduced as a sport in Sydney 2000 nearly all the positive tests that occurred in both Sydney (10 out of 11) and Athens (6 out of 10) four years later were in powerlifting. This caused those in charge of the sport to severely tighten up the rules on doping and it is satisfying to see that although three powerlifters were caught in Beijing the number of positive tests has been reduced dramatically. Table 7.2 breaks the 27 positive doping tests that have been found at Summer Paralympic Games down by continental affiliation and gender of the athletes concerned. It can clearly be seen that the majority of positive tests have occurred with athletes from Europe and Asia and that 89 per cent of all positive tests were from male athletes.

Study activity

List possible reasons why the prevalence of positive doping tests at the Paralympic Games is so much higher for European nations. Make a second list of possible reasons why the prevalence of positive doping tests at the Paralympic Games is so much higher for men than women.

Therapeutic use exemption (TUE)

Given the nature of some impairments certain individuals may be required to take substances or use treatment methods, under doctors orders, that are prohibited by the WADA code. Under such circumstances, if the individual wishes to continue competing in their chosen sport, they must apply to

Table 7.2 Positive Paralympic Games doping tests by continental association and gender since Barcelona, 1992

	Africa	Americas	Asia	Europe	Oceania	Total	Male	Female
Barcelona, 1992	0	1	0	2	0	3	3	0
Atlanta, 1996	0	0	0	0	0	0	0	0
Sydney, 2000	1	1	3	6	0	11	10	1
Athens, 2004	0	1	3	6	0	10	9	1
Beijing, 2008	1	0	1	1	0	3	2	1
Total	2	3	7	15	0	27	24	3

either the IPC TUE Committee or their own national anti-doping agency for a therapeutic use exemption certificate at the latest on the final day of entry for the competition they wish to compete in. However, in extraordinary circumstances, such as an injury during training or illness just prior to competition an emergency TUE may be granted. The TUE Committee to which the application has been made, and consisting of at least three members, then evaluates the request in accordance with the WADA International Standards for Therapeutic Use Exemptions and renders a decision. This decision is then communicated to both the athlete and WADA. At this point WADA may, at the request of the athlete concerned or of their own volition, review the decision and, in exceptional circumstances may even overturn it. The outcome of this is that an athlete who is granted a TUE may then compete in a sporting competition and if drug tested the testers will know to expect to find the allowed banned substance in the sample and the expected levels of that substance.

Study activity

Make a list of possible reasons why there have been so few positive doping tests at Winter Paralympic Games when compared to their Summer Paralympic and Winter Olympic counterparts.

Boosting

Boosting is the colloquial terminology for self-induced autonomic dysreflexia, which is considered as a performance enhancing technique (Harris, 1994). Boosting refers to a technique potentially employed by athletes with a spinal cord injury at the T6 level or above. The resultant affect is similar to that produced by ergogenic aids. Boosting has, therefore, been banned in sport for the disabled. Reported methods for boosting by some athletes include temporarily blocking their own urinary catheter, drinking large amounts of fluids prior to their event to distend the bladder, tightening clothing, and sitting for long periods of time. According to Grey-Thompson (2008) it can boost performance by up to 25 per cent. Potential complications of prolonged boosting are the same as for non-self-induced autonomic dysreflexia in general e.g. stroke, seizure, irregular heart rhythm, heart attack, and potentially death (Malanga, 2008). Boosting is, therefore, banned not just on ethical grounds, but also health grounds.

Classification

The most obvious and clear cut case of cheating the classification system occurred in Sydney in the intellectually disabled basketball. This case is described in much greater detail in Chapter 10. However, given that in Beijing there were ninety-nine functional reclassifications, sixty-three visual impairment reclassifications and thirteen athletes reclassified again after their first appearance in front of the classifiers it clearly shows that classification is not an exact science. Two athletes were actually reclassified to such an extent that they were deemed to be not sufficiently disabled enough to compete in Paralympic sport, one of them after having won a silver medal. The inexactness of the classification system clearly opens up opportunities for individuals to try and get themselves classified into a group that would give them a competitive advantage or to be simply wrongly classified and the mistake not get spotted.

Tampering with technology

Grey-Thompson (2008) claims that there have been instances where wheelchair track athletes have felt that their racing chairs, and in particular their compensators which they calibrate themselves to help them go around the two bends on the track, have been tampered with. A slight change in the calibration might mean that the chair would either not turn in correctly, forcing the chair out wide, or might turn in too sharply causing the chair to hit the kerb on the inside of the track. For this reason Grey-Thompson claims she guarded her racing chair very closely whenever she was racing.

Technological doping or cyborg athlete syndrome

With the massive improvements in performance standards currently occurring in disability sport some athletes have reached a standard that might allow them to qualify for the Olympic Games. However, the technology they use in terms of adapted equipment in order to enable them to compete has raised questions regarding advantages such equipment might give them over their non-disabled counterparts. This has led to the coining of such terms as 'technological doping' or 'cyborg athlete'. The most notable example of this is, of course, Oscar Pistorius, the South African double-below the knee amputee who uses carbon fibre blade prosthetic limbs to allow him to compete. It is unnecessary to go into detail regarding the Pistorius case as it has been covered heavily by both the media and academics worldwide (see Wolbring, 2008; Howe, 2008), However, in brief, Pistorius, a Paralympic Gold medallist and world record holder decided he wished to compete against non-disabled athletes in open competition and if possible qualify to compete in the 400 metres at the Olympic Games in Beijing. He came within half a second of the qualifying standard, when in March 2007 the IAAF introduced a rule regarding 'technical aids' that brought into question the use of such prosthetic limbs within the Olympic Games as it was felt they gave the user an unfair advantage when compared to the capabilities of the human leg. Following an appeal to the Court of Arbitration for Sport (CAS), which challenged the veracity of the tests carried out by the IOC and the IAAF it was decided by CAS that Pistorius should be allowed compete (but only using the technology which he used in the original tests). In the end Pistorius failed to reach the qualifying time for the individual event, but still hoped to make his country's relay team, at which point the IAAF Secretary General Pierre Weiss is cited as saying 'we'd prefer that they don't select him for reasons of safety . . . Pistorius will risk the physical safety of himself and other athletes if he runs in the main pack of the relay event' (CBC Sports, 2008). In the end Pistorius was not selected for the South African team as four other athletes posted faster times. Another South African, swimmer Natalie Du Toit, a single leg amputee, did qualify to represent South Africa in the 10 km open water swimming event at the Beijing Olympic Games and there was no such reticence to her participation by either the IOC or FINA, as she does not use any kind of prosthetic when she swims, although she does for daily living.

The fear then, in the case of Pistorius, for the IOC and the IAAF, was not the usual prejudice most people with disabilities have encountered at some point in their lives of being considered 'less than human', but in fact the complete opposite – the fear of being 'more than human'. The very devices society has devised to allow individuals to walk in the upright position like everyone else and to compete in running events in a similar style and manner as their non-disabled counterparts are now considered to give an unfair competitive advantage. Pistorius has gone from a fine Paralympic athlete whose achievements were to be applauded, perhaps in the slightly patronising manner outlined in the previous chapter, to a kind of 'Robocop' of the track who might not only have an unfair advantage over athletes not wearing his prosthetic limbs, but also might reap danger and injury upon both himself and his fellow relay competitors. Swartz and Watermeyer (2008) ascribe this reaction to the fact that Pistorius is effectively challenging one of the key underlying ethics' of sport – that of bodily perfection. He is challenging culturally ascribed definitions of bodily perfection based around non-disabled conceptions. To have someone whose body is less than perfect (i.e. missing limbs) potentially beating athletes whose bodies far more readily meet the requirements laid down for bodily perfection is a challenge to the virtues of those who hold power, especially when that body has been 'technologically accessorised' with prosthetic limbs. It is somewhat ironic that the term 'prosthetic' is derived from the Greek meaning 'an addition designed to remove physical stigma' (Howe, 2008, p. 127), when in Pistorius' case it appears to have resulted in removing the stigma of being disabled whilst adding the stigma of being 'more than human' in athletic ability, but 'less than human' in physical appearance i.e. some kind of cyborg. This then begins to raise numerous questions around the difference between being human and being a machine. Whether Pistorius ever finally gets his wish to compete in the Olympic Games or not remains to be seen, but what is certain is that the questions raised by the issues related to his attempted participation will be far reaching and will continue to be debated for a long time to come.

Conclusion

It is clear that the Paralympic Movement has some highly complex and difficult issues to deal with. How it deals with these issues and how their remedies are perceived will ultimately decide the success or failure of the movement. Many of the issues such as doping have been a problem for the Olympic Movement for many years and so hopefully IPC can learn from the mistakes and triumphs of the IOC in this area. Clearly, as the Paralympic Games become more successful and gain more media coverage the pressure on some individuals to cheat will increase. In addition, how IPC deals with the move towards an elite sporting model, thus moving it further away from its cultural model roots, will potentially impact upon its ability to successfully serve all the members of the Paralympic community, particularly women and athletes with high support needs.

Chapter review questions

1 What are the differences between a cultural and a sports event? Give examples of each.
2 Should athletes with disabilities who compete at the Paralympic Games be called Olympians or Paralympians? Give reasons for your answer.
3 What extra issues are involved in doping control within sport for the disabled and how are they managed?
4 Name and explain the different classification methods used in sport for the disabled.
5 Should Oscar Pistorius have been banned from non-disabled competition?
6 How are Oscar Pistorius's blades different from the latest aerodynamic carbon fibre racing bike or technologically enhanced swimming suit?

Suggested further reading

Sherrill, C. (ed.), 1999, Disability Sport, Classification and Sport/Leisure Learning, *Adapted Physical Activity Quarterly* (special edition), Vol. 16(3), pp. 206–330.

8 The under representation of women and athletes with high support needs at the Paralympic Games

Chapter aims

- Describe the development of the participation of women in the Summer and Winter Paralympic Games.
- Highlight the role of gender on participation in sport for the disabled.
- Describe the development of the participation of athletes with high support needs in the Summer and Winter Paralympic Games.
- Highlight the declining numbers of athletes with high support needs participating in the recent Summer and Winter Paralympic Games with possible reasons for decline.

Point four of the IPC Mission Statement that begins 'The Mission that provides the broad goals to the IPC for a long-term strategy is ...' reads 'To develop opportunities for women athletes and athletes with high support needs in sport at all levels and in all structures' (IPC Website, 2009c). The fact that the IPC Mission Statement deems it necessary to specifically include these two groups of athletes, and the fact that both groups have their own standing committee within the IPC governance structure, highlights the fact that they are the two groups of athletes within the Paralympic family that are hardest hit by many of the issues raised in the earlier chapters. This chapter will look in a little more detail at each of these groups to see why this might be and how the impact of these issues might manifest themselves for each group.

Women at the Paralympic Games

Table 8.1 highlights the increasing numbers of participants in both the Summer and Winter Paralympic Games since their inception in 1960 and 1976 respectively. It also shows this participation by gender, which highlights the much greater male participation levels relative to women. In terms of the Summer Games the table clearly demonstrates the growth in Paralympic participation over the last five games as well as the steady increase in women's participation at the Games relative to their male counterparts. The

Table 8.1 Participation by gender at the Paralympic Games

Year	Location	Men	Women	Total
1960	Rome, Italy	NA	NA	~ 400
1964	Tokyo, Japan	309	66	375
1968	Tel Aviv, Israel	554	176	730
1972	Heidelberg, West Germany	722	273	995
1976	Örnsköldsvik, Sweden	161	37	198
1976	Toronto, Canada	1404	253	1657
1980	Geilo, Norway	229	70	299
1980	Arnhem, The Netherlands	1539	472	2011
1984	Innsbruck, Austria	325	94	419
1984	Stoke Mandeville, UK & New York, USA	NA	NA	1100 1800
1988	Innsbruck, Austria	300	77	377
1988	Seoul, South Korea	2503	710	3213
1992	Tignes-Albertville, France	288	77	365
1992	Barcelona, Spain & Madrid, Spain	2323 NA	697 NA	3020 ~1400
1994	Lillehammer, Norway	381	90	471
1996	Atlanta, USA	2415	780	3195
1998	Nagano, Japan	440	121	561
2000	Sydney, Australia	2867	978	3843
2002	Salt Lake, USA	329	87	416
2004	Athens, Greece	2646	1160	3806
2006	Torino, Italy	375	99	474
2008	Beijing, P.R. China	2584	1367	3951

(NA: Data not currently available)

drop in male participation at the Athens and Beijing Games is likely due to the efforts by the International Paralympic Committee (IPC) to encourage greater participation by women at the games and is possibly compounded by the 4,000 athlete cap placed on participation at the Paralympic Games through the co-operative agreement signed between IPC and the IOC.

The Summer Paralympic Games

Women's historical participation rates at the Summer Olympic and Paralympic Games are shown as a percentage of the total number of participants in Figure 8.1. As can be seen there have been times when the percentage for women at the Paralympics has been higher than that for women at the Olympics in the same year. However, this is probably due more to the much lower overall number of participants competing at the Paralympics at that time. What is clear is that the numbers of women at both Games has been steadily increasing relative to the number of men, especially over the last twenty years. This may be an indication that some of the IOC/IPC strategies for increasing female participation are beginning to take effect. This is possibly also an indication of the increasing importance and recognition of women's

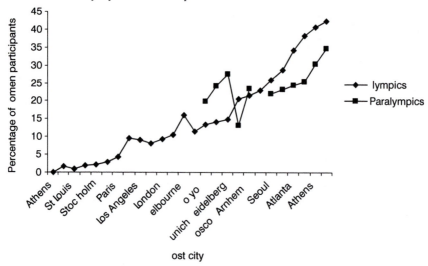

Figure 8.1 A comparison of female participation rates at the Summer Olympic and Paralympic games

sport over the last twenty years. The higher overall starting levels for women at the Paralympics is more likely a reflection of the period in history when they began. The fact that the percentage for women at the Olympics is so much higher than that for women at the Paralympics in Beijing 2008 is indicative of the extra difficulties faced by women with disabilities to get involved in and reach the highest levels in sport.

The Winter Paralympic Games

Women's historical participation rates at the Winter Olympic and Paralympic Games are shown as a percentage of the total number of participants in Figure 8.2 . Whilst participation rates for women at the Winter Olympic Games have risen steadily with time, those for women at the Paralympics have remained virtually static at around 20 per cent since the Winter Paralympic Games commenced in 1976. There is almost no research whatsoever regarding the participation of women at the Winter Paralympic Games, but it is likely that the reason for this consistently low participation of women is due to a combination of factors including cost, the fact that the only team sport (sledge hockey) is totally male dominated (thus increasing the number of males relative to females), the differing risk-taking propensities of men and women (men do riskier sports as described below) and geographical location to mountains or indoor ice rinks around the world.

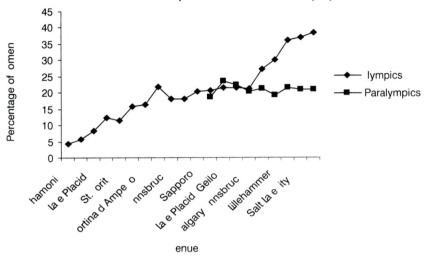

Figure 8.2 A comparison of female participation rates at the Winter Olympic and Paralympic games

The role of gender in participation at the Paralympic Games

Gender appears to play a key role in participation rates amongst persons with disabilities. This can be partially accounted for by the fact that the 1980 national census in America revealed that more men are permanently injured through accidents while more women have chronic disabling conditions that are not accident related (Grimes and French, 1987). Thierfeld and Gibbons (1986) showed that in competitive sports considerably fewer women are involved than men. They suggest that this is due to the fact that men do more dangerous things. They are more daring, have more accidents and become disabled. However, according to many authors, the problem goes much deeper than that. Huang (2005), Olenik (1998) and Guthrie (1999), to name but a few, all discuss the problems persons with disabilities, and women with disabilities in particular, face in any attempts to become involved in any kind of sporting activity. These include:

1   Generally men grow up playing sport and are encouraged to do so by everyone around them. Women, however, generally do not and are not encouraged to do so. This is equally true of non-disabled girls and women and so if they are not encouraged, young women with disabilities are even less likely to be.

2   It is rare for women who were not active in sports prior to becoming disabled to turn to them afterwards for fitness, especially as those who influence them are unlikely to encourage them in that direction.

3   Disabled women and girls often face enormous emotional problems. Issues of low self- esteem, lack of experience in sports, fear of success and failure, which are already documented for non-disabled women are even greater problems for women with disabilities.
4   A lack of role models to counteract rolelessness plays a major part as they provide tangible proof of what is attainable. This is compounded by a lack of media coverage of disability in general and disability sport in particular.
5   There is a lack of adequate coaching within disability sport in general and what there is is often monopolised by the male athletes.
6   There is a lack of opportunities to take part in disability sport and often a lack of awareness of what little provision there is.
7   Women, even more than men, with disabilities often struggle to find employment and so without the material resources to support themselves survival becomes the key concern, making it unlikely that they will have the time, energy or financial wherewithal to take part in recreational or sporting activities.

Interestingly, studies by both Brittain (2002) and Olenik (1998) came to the conclusion that once athletes with disabilities had reached the elite level the problems they encounter in maintaining their participation become much more about the structure of the sport they are involved in and those charged with running and administering it.

Economics plays a major role in deciding the likelihood of a disabled individual becoming involved in sport. Studies such as Hargreaves (2000) and Kolkka and Williams (1997) have shown that economics is a major barrier to participation in sport, especially for women with disabilities. Lonsdale (1990) found that women with disabilities are at a far greater economic disadvantage than their male counterparts in employment and in the distribution of state benefits or other financial support. According to Smith and Twomey (2002) 44 per cent of disabled men compared with 52 per cent of disabled women in Britain were economically inactive in 2001 in contrast with 9 per cent of non-disabled men and 21 per cent of non-disabled women. Huang (2005), citing the Taiwan Federation for the Disabled (2001) and Kuao (2001), claims that in Taiwan in the same year 87 per cent of disabled women and 77 per cent of disabled men were economically inactive. Without the financial wherewithal to take care of the daily necessities of life it is unlikely that any individual will take up a recreational or sporting pastime.

Women's participation at the Beijing Paralympic Games

This section will use data from the last six Paralympic Games, which appears to indicate that women's participation at the Summer Paralympic Games is increasing worldwide. The left hand side of Table 8.2 shows the top five sports

Table 8.2 Top and bottom five sports for female participation in Beijing by gender and sport and as a percentage of all women participating at the Games

Percentage of women by gender and sport				Percentage of all participating women by sport			
Highest		Lowest		Highest		Lowest	
Sport	%	Sport	%	Sport	%	Sport	%
Equestrianism	68.5	Wheelchair rugby	3.4	Athletics	24.3	Wheelchair rugby	0.2
Rowing	48.1	Sailing	16.3	Swimming	16.4	Sailing	1.0
Sitting volleyball	47.0	Cycling	25.9	Wheelchair basketball	8.8	Wheelchair fencing	1.8
Wheelchair basketball	45.5	Wheelchair fencing	28.6	Table tennis	7.0	Boccia	1.9
Swimming	40.0	Boccia	29.5	Sitting volleyball	6.2	Wheelchair tennis	2.6

that women competed in at the Beijing Paralympic Games when compared to male participation in the same sport. Of the twenty sports competed in at Beijing, women only outnumbered men in one – equestrianism. Of the remaining four sports in the top five, two of them are team sports. This may, therefore, not be a true reflection of women's participation in these sports relative to men as the number of teams and the number of players per team is fixed by the organisers. The other two sports in the top five are rowing and swimming. Swimming is often used as a rehabilitative tool for people with disabilities and doesn't require much in the way of specialist equipment, which might explain why the number of women relative to men is so much higher than for other individual sports. Rowing, which was making its debut at the Paralympic Games in Beijing, had a limited number of events and competitors and as such this may have led to an artificial reflection of the number of women with disabilities taking part in rowing. All of the five sports with the lowest percentage of women relative to men, with the exception of sailing, are individual sports and/or require both specialist equipment and training, which as indicated earlier are often monopolised by male athletes.

The right hand side of Table 8.2 shows the top five sports that women competed in relative to the total number of female participants at the Beijing Paralympic Games. This clearly shows that athletics and swimming are by far the two most popular sports for women. However, this is not particularly surprising as they are also the two biggest sports for men and women at both the Olympic and Paralympic Games. The high percentage of women participating in these two sports at the Paralympics is likely a reflection of the popularity, availability and accessibility of these two sports worldwide. Of the five sports with the lowest percentage of women taking part relative to other sports four of them are highly technical sports necessitating expensive equipment and coaching, which put them beyond the reach of many disabled athletes' means. This is especially true for women, whom as seen in the previous section suffer from multiple barriers of various kinds when trying to access sporting opportunities. The fifth sport, boccia, is for athletes with severe disabilities, now called athletes with high support needs. When combining a severe disability with all of the issues previously outlined it is hardly surprising that so few women with high support needs compete at the Paralympic Games.

A further investigation of the most popular sport for women in Beijing, athletics, shows that there have been some big changes in participation numbers for women between the Athens Paralympic Games in 2004 and the Beijing Games four years later. The number of women competing in athletics in Beijing rose to 332 in four disability categories from 298 in Athens. At the same time the number of men competing in athletics dropped from 766 in Athens to 696 in Beijing. In addition the number of medal events in athletics dropped from 194 (137 male, 57 female) in Athens to 160 (100 male, 60 female) in Beijing. It may seem odd that the number of women competing rose and the number of medal events dropped in Beijing (as it had four years previously in Athens), but the following quote from Fiona (in Huang, 2005) may give a clue to a possible reason why:

> There just aren't enough females in the sport anyway. And you have got the different disabilities in different classes so in actual fact it's easier for women to get to the top than it is for men because there are fewer female athletes, especially in paraplegics ... So for me I picked the right thing because there wasn't much competition really, so I was lucky, you know more chance of a medal and travelling to represent Britain or England.
>
> (Fiona, in Huang, 2005, p. 148)

Fiona, who competed as a shot putter in Sydney, appears to intimate that because there are fewer women taking part in sport and in her sport of athletics in particular, it was far easier for her to be chosen and improved her chances of getting a medal. In an attempt to improve standards of competition the International Paralympic Committee and the organising committees in both Beijing and Athens cut back on the number of medal events for both men and women in an attempt to increase the number of participants per event and improve standards. In three events for women (javelin, discus and shot-put) the organisers also combined the classes for the highest categories of disability in the spinal cord injured and cerebral palsied disability groupings.

The number of countries competing in athletics rose from 103 in Sydney to 115 in Athens, but in Beijing this number dropped slightly to 111. The number of countries entering female participants in athletics, which had risen quite dramatically from fifty-five in Sydney to eighty in Athens, dropped back down to sixty-six in Beijing. The number of countries entering only male athletes dropped from forty-eight in Sydney to thirty-five in Athens, which would appear to indicate that opportunities for disabled women to take part in disability athletics worldwide were apparently on the increase. However, rather worryingly, this number rose dramatically in Beijing to fifty-five. Therefore, although the number of women taking part in athletics in Beijing had risen this increase was due to a much smaller number of nations bringing more women, with almost half the countries having no women at all. This is likely the result of a combination of factors. The decreasing number of spaces and medal events for men (thus increasing competition for places amongst male athletes in each nation), and the lack of opportunities for women to get involved and progress to the elite level, particularly in economically under-developed countries, possibly resulted in these countries only sending men and the more economically developed nations being able to enter more women than was previously possible.

It would appear, however, from the following data that the number of women taking part in the Paralympic Games is on the increase worldwide. Figure 8.3 shows the breakdown in participation of women at the last six Paralympic games by continental association. Although this clearly demonstrates that, historically, the majority of female participants at the games have come from Europe and the Americas, it is also clear that the participation of women in the other three continents is definitely on the increase.

Overall, the number of countries entering no female athletes at the Paralympic Games appears to be on the decline. Table 8.3 shows the percentage of National Paralympic Committees (NPCs) from each continental association, relative to the total number of NPCs, that had no

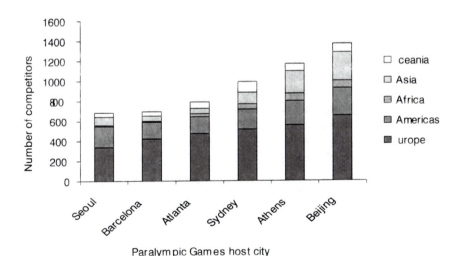

Figure 8.3 Female participation at the Paralympic Games by Continental Association over the last twenty years

Table 8.3 Percentage of NPC's by continental affiliation with no female participants in relation to the total number of teams with no female participants over the last 20 years

	Seoul	Barcelona	Atlanta	Sydney	Athens	Beijing
Europe (EOC)	26.7	19.4	19.1	15.8	16.1	10.4
Americas (PASO)	20	22.6	19.1	15.8	16.1	18.8
Africa (ANOCA)	20	29	25.5	18.4	19.4	31.3
Asia (OCA)	33.3	29	38.3	42.1	48.4	31.3
Oceania (ONOC)	0	0	2	7.9	0	8.3

female participants at the last six Paralympic Games. Up to the Athens 2004 Games, with the exception of Asia, the general trend clearly demonstrated a decrease in countries entering no women at the Paralympic Games from four of the continents. However, in Beijing two noteworthy changes occurred in these figures. Firstly, the percentage of African nations bringing no women to the Games rose sharply. This coincides with the participation of a number of African nations in the Paralympic Games for the first time, possibly as a result of the development work IPC and other agencies have been doing in Africa (see IPC website, 2009g). Many of these nations only brought very small teams and possibly due to a combination of factors such as economics, lack of development of female sporting opportunities etc, chose to bring male athletes. The other change of note is the apparent decrease in Asian NPCs not taking women to Beijing. In reality the number of NPCs from Asia not taking women to Beijing remained the same as in Athens, but the large increase in NPCs from Africa and a slight increase in Oceania and the Americas not taking women to Beijing meant the figure for Asia dropped in overall terms.

Figure 8.4 looks in slightly closer detail at the participation of NPCs from Asia at the last six Paralympic games and highlights the fact that the number of countries participating at the games from Asia has nearly trebled over this period. It can be seen that the number of Asian countries with no female participants has dropped slightly over the last three Games.

In line with Sherrill's (1997) findings regarding the Atlanta Paralympic Games the vast majority of all countries not sending female participants to Beijing had team sizes of less than nine and the lack of female participants in these teams probably reflect economic limitations, possibly with an underlying bias towards male sport and a lack of opportunities for women. When comparing the same countries' participation at the Beijing Olympic Games it is found that all countries in continents other than Asia and thirteen of the fifteen countries in Asia who had no female participants at the Paralympics did have female participants at the Olympic Games. Their lack of female participation at the Paralympics may be due to a lack of development of disability sport within these countries, possibly exacerbated by cultural issues around disability and gender. Of the remaining two Asian countries, Saudi Arabia and Qatar (both strongly Muslim states) had no

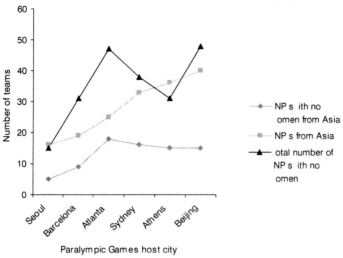

Figure 8.4 Asian NPC participation at the Paralympic Games over the last twenty years

women at the Olympic or Paralympic Games despite fielding a total of thirty-four men at the Olympics and five at the Paralympics. This appears to highlight the possibility of another barrier to female participation in sport – that of religious and cultural issues. However, it should be pointed out that in Athens there were five countries from Asia in this situation who fielded a total of thirty-seven men at the Athens Olympics and twenty at the Athens Paralympics, so it would appear that things are possibly changing. In fact one country, Kuwait, who fielded eight men and zero women at the Beijing Olympics actually included one woman in their team of eight at the Beijing Paralympic Games.

Although participation rates for both female Olympic and Paralympic participants are steadily increasing relative to their male counterparts there are many issues relating to opportunity, prejudice and body image that are still preventing disabled females from getting involved in sport and reaching the highest levels. These barriers may also be exacerbated by political, cultural and religious issues relating to women's role expectations within a specific society. It would appear from the data that the participation of women at the Summer Paralympic Games is on the increase with more countries entering female athletes. There are still many differences, however, between continents and even between sports and there is still a long way to go before anything like equity is reached.

Study activity

Select a couple of major issues highlighted above that impact upon participation of women with disabilities around the world in sport at the highest level and try to design strategies relevant to each issue that might assist in helping these women overcome them.

Athletes with high support needs

Originally called athletes with severe disabilities, the term 'severe disability' led to concerns that it was laden with overly negative connotations that might prove detrimental to those involved. The new terminology of athletes with high support needs (AHSN) was, therefore, introduced in order to emphasise the support needs that all athletes require to make it to the very top in their sport (coaching, financial, etc.), whilst recognising that some athletes with disabilities have higher and possibly more specialised support needs than others. Such support might include a sighted guide for a blind athlete, both for in and out of competition assistance at a Paralympic Games where the built environment will be unfamiliar to the athlete and they may also need a guide to compete in events such as track events. There are two broad categories of AHSN – those with more severe physical disabilities and those who are blind or visually impaired to such an extent that they need a guide to assist them, not only for their sport, but for their everyday living needs. Although the many developments in classification over the years, combined with incomplete record keeping in the early years of the Paralympic Games, has meant that it is very difficult to trace accurately the participation of AHSN in the Games it is known that the first events for tetraplegic athletes were added to the programme in Tokyo, 1964. AHSN with other physical disabilities and blind and visually impaired AHSN did not take part in the Summer Paralympic Games until Toronto, 1976. Some authors claim that there were demonstration events for blind athletes in Heidelberg, 1972, but no records of these can be found and the Director of Sports for these Games, Joerg Schmeckl, has no recollection of them (Schmeckl, 2008, personal communication).

The squeeze on athlete numbers at the Paralympic Games

Following the introduction of athletes with amputations and visual impairments the total number of medals awarded in Toronto, 1876 rose from 575 at Heidelberg (1972) to 1,172 at Toronto. With the addition of athletes with cerebral palsy in Arnhem four years later the total number awarded rose to 1,601. The split site Games of 1984 in Stoke Mandeville, UK and Long Island, New York, as well as the addition of Les Autres athletes to the Games in New York, effectively allowed for more athletes and more events at each venue and the total number of medals awarded at both venues combined hit an all-time high of 2,767. In Seoul, 1988 with the Games finally returning to the Olympic host city and re-combining into one event the number of medals awarded dropped back to 2,208. This return to the Olympic host city, which has continued ever since, combined with a number of other issues and events appear to have had quite a major impact on the participation of AHSN in the years that followed. These issues and events include:

- Having the Games at the same host city venues as the Olympic Games very shortly after the Olympic Games allowed for direct comparison. For example, due to the classification system used in Seoul there were twenty-one male and fourteen female 100 m finals in athletics compared to one for each gender at the Olympic Games. In addition many of the events were straight finals with no heats necessary due to the limited number of athletes within a particular classification grouping. This led to the perception amongst some that athletes only had to turn up at the Games to win a medal, which was totally at odds with the elite sporting model the movement had already begun moving towards.
- In January 1987, at an ICC meeting in Seoul, the Seoul Paralympic Co-ordinating Committee (SPOC) had tried to get the number of athletes and Officials, previously agreed at 4,000, cut to a total of 3,000, citing financial and facility issues as the reason. Although this cut did not actually occur in the end, it is clear from the minutes that a formula had been devised to cut the number of athletes if necessary. The additional financial burden on Olympic host cities of also hosting the Paralympic Games would continue to be a source of pressure on the number of athletes allowed to participate in subsequent Games.
- As part of the ongoing move towards an elite sport model minimum entry standards for Paralympic Games had already been in use since at least Arnhem, 1980.

The combination of these three issues came to a real head for the first time in Barcelona, 1992. In an attempt to reduce the number of medals awarded and overcome the perception that an individual only had to turn up to win a medal, a functional classification system was introduced in six sports for CP-ISRA, ISOD and ISMWSF athletes. According to Sherrill (1993) the balance of power between these three organisations and the way qualifying standards were worked out prevented many countries from taking CP athletes to Barcelona. This, in turn, impacted on other events due to the rule that an event had to contain athletes from at least three countries and two continents to be considered viable. This resulted in events either being integrated with others or deleted from the programme completely. The total number of medals awarded in Barcelona fell by over 500 from the previous Games to 1,503. By Beijing, 2008 this number had dropped to 1,431.

Athletes with high support needs and the squeeze on athlete numbers

Athletes with high support needs by definition require greater support in order to participate in their chosen sport. This means that they face far more barriers to getting involved in and reaching the elite level in their chosen sport, than their more functionally able counterparts. Add to this that there are probably less of them worldwide to start with and it is unsurprising that the number of AHSN making it to the elite level in sport is relatively small compared to the number of athletes with a disability as a whole. Therefore, when events such as those that happened in Barcelona occur, it is usually the events for AHSN that are hardest hit by deletions or being combined with more functionally able athletes thereby negating any possible chance they might have had of a medal. This in turn negatively impacts on the motivation of these athletes to continue to train and compete, which can lead to even fewer AHSN being available to compete in future events (Wilhite, 2002). Several events have occurred over the last couple of decades in order to try and counteract the perceived decreasing opportunities for AHSN to take part in the Paralympic Games. These include the setting up of a standing committee within IPC in 2004 to specifically look out for the welfare and needs of AHSN within the Paralympic family. In addition sports for specific groups of AHSN such as boccia (CP athletes) and wheelchair rugby

Plate 8.1 Boccia is a Paralympic sport specifically for Cerebral Palsied athletes with high support needs

(tetraplegic athletes) were added to the Paralympic programme in order to provide opportunities for these athletes.

However, even with sports such as wheelchair rugby, which is specifically for AHSN, some are concerned that the most severely disabled are being overlooked in the pursuit of sporting excellence and success. Players in wheelchair rugby are given a points score (0.5 – most disabled to 3.5 – least disabled) with each team only allowed to have four players totalling no more than eight points on the field at any one time. Schreiner and Strohkendl (2006) claim that wheelchair rugby is dominated on field by high point players (3–3.5 points) due to the fact that the eight point team limit favours their inclusion and that this has led to the continuous decline of low point players within the sport in recent years. This clearly demonstrates the tension within the Paralympic movement of trying to move towards an elite sporting model that matches societal perceptions and understandings of what sport should look like, and providing sporting opportunities at the elite level for all their constituent members. One more issue for AHSN in this area raised by Lepore *et al.* (2007) is the perception by some AHSN that they do not really feel welcome by the more functionally able athletes at the Paralympic Games. Lepore *et al.* (2007, p. 271) state that 'Athletes with more severe disabilities feel that the more elite athletes with disabilities are embarrassed to compete at the same Games as them'. This is a perception that seems at least partially borne out by the quotation in Chapter 5 by Ina quoted in Brittain (2004) where she claims to be embarrassed to have had to travel on the same aeroplane as the boccia players. This not only highlights that disabled people are just as capable of being disablist as anyone else, but also is another possible reason why so few AHSN feel motivated enough to try and make it to the elite level in sport. However, it should also be pointed out that the very wording of the quotation above by Lepore *et al.* (2007) smacks of the very same disablist undertones in that it describes the athletes that supposedly are embarrassed to compete alongside AHSN as 'more elite' rather than more functionally able. This, therefore, clearly aligns elitism with relative functional ability i.e. the more functionally able a person is (stronger, higher, faster) the more 'elite' they are considered.

Athletes with high support needs in Beijing, 2008

Table 8.4 shows the distribution of AHSN by continental association at the Beijing Paralympic Games, as well as splitting the totals into physical disabilities and blind athletes who require a guide. This highlights one final issue with regard to opportunities for AHSN to participate in the Paralympic Games, that of the ability of their relevant NPC to afford to provide the necessary extra support (guide, carer, etc.) needed by an individual AHSN. Given the choice between taking an extra athlete or paying for a guide or a carer to accompany an AHSN, NPCs on tight budgets are more likely to take another more functionally able athlete in order to increase their chances

Table 8.4 Distribution of athletes with high support needs by continental association at the Beijing 2008 Paralympic Games

	All AHSN				*Physical disabilities*				*Blind*			
	NPCs	*M*	*W*	*T*	*NPCs*	*M*	*W*	*T*	*NPCs*	*M*	*W*	*T*
Africa	6	15	4	19	3	7	4	11	4	8	0	8
Asia	15	125	39	164	10	69	22	91	12	56	17	73
Americas	14	104	34	138	12	63	24	87	7	41	10	51
Europe	34	250	81	331	30	163	56	219	26	87	25	112
Oceania	2	32	13	45	2	27	10	37	2	5	3	8
Total	71	526	171	697	57	329	116	445	51	197	55	252

of gaining medals – on which most NPCs' future funding is based. This is, of course, also partly dependent upon the how many places the Delegation Quota System (DQS) employed by IPC allows a particular country to take up at a particular Games. The DQS does allow for NPCs to take additional staff to a Games to meet the additional needs of AHSN, but this is also dependent upon the NPC being able to afford the additional staff necessary. It is clear from Table 8.4 that the majority of AHSN at the Beijing Paralympic Games came from the more economically developed western nations.

In total, AHSN made up 17.6 per cent of all athletes who participated in Beijing. However, only one quarter of the AHSN were female, again highlighting the impact of potential multiple discrimination i.e. being a woman and having a disability and having a disability that requires a high level of support. Unfortunately there is no other accurate data available to allow for a comparison of participation at previous Paralympic Games, but estimates by IPC cite figures of 24.3 per cent for Sydney and 23.5 per cent for Athens (IPC, 2008, personal communication), which if anywhere near correct display a worrying downward trend in the participation of AHSN at Summer Paralympic Games. The estimates for Winter Games cite figures of 10.6 per cent for Salt Lake City and 7.6 per cent for Turin (IPC, 2008, personal communication), again displaying the same downward trend and possibly the even greater problems and issues involved for an AHSN to become involved in Winter sports.

Study activity

What do you think needs to be done to encourage more athletes with high support needs to become involved in sport at the highest level? How would you go about enabling this whilst still trying to meet all the other aims of the IPC?

Conclusion

As can be seen from the above information participation rates for Women at the Summer Paralympic Games appear to be on the increase, although they are still well below those of their non-disabled counterparts. Contrastingly, however, the participation rates for women at the Winter Paralympic Games have remained virtually stagnant since the Games began over thirty years ago and participation rates for athletes with high support needs actually appear to be on the decline. As outlined above there are numerous, and often complex, possible reasons for this that can vary greatly from country to country and culture to culture. What is very clear is that IPC and those involved in organising disability sport worldwide have a long and difficult task ahead of them if they are to overcome these issues and greatly increase the presence of women and athletes with high support needs at both the Summer and Winter Paralympic Games.

Chapter review questions

1 List and explain some of the issues for women wishing to become involved in sport for the disabled.
2 Participation rates for women with disabilities at the Winter Paralympics have remained virtually unchanged for over thirty years. What are some of the possible reasons for this?
3 What is an 'athlete with a high support need'?
4 What are some of the possible reasons for the apparent downward trend in the participation of athletes with high support needs at both the Summer and Winter Paralympic Games?

Suggested further reading

Lonsdale S., 1990, *Women and Disability: The Experience of Physical Disability Among Women*, Macmillan, London, UK.
Wendell, S., 1996, *The Rejected Body: Feminist Phiolosophical Reflections on Disability*, Routledge, London, UK.

9 International perspectives on Paralympic participation

Chapter aims

- Outline the differences in participation rates by continent in the Summer and Winter Paralympic Games.
- Highlight the most successful nations in terms of medal success at the Summer and Winter Paralympic Games.
- Raise a variety of issues from an international perspective that impact upon participation and success at the Summer and Winter Paralympic Games.

The aim of this chapter is to look at participation in the Summer and Winter Paralympic Games from a global perspective and to highlight a variety of issues that impact upon participation and success at the Games. As highlighted in Chapter 3, membership of the International Paralympic Committee (IPC) is divided into the same five regional areas as those used by the International Olympic Committee (Africa, the Americas, Asia, Europe and Oceania). There are currently 161 National Paralympic Committees in membership with IPC, compared with 204 National Olympic Committees. This chapter will look at participation in the Summer and Winter Paralympic Games on a regional basis in order to highlight certain disparities in participation that become clear from the figures. It will then take each region individually and give short 'snapshots' from a couple of different countries within those regions in order to highlight a range of different issues that might impact on participation either nationally, regionally or internationally. Finally, throughout the chapter attempts will be made to highlight and explain some of the possible reasons between different participation levels at the Summer and Winter Games.

This chapter begins by showing a comparison of participation by current IPC member nations at the Summer and Winter Paralympic Games. Table 9.1 shows that, of the 161 member nations of IPC, 153 of those nations (95 per cent) have competed at a Summer Paralympic Games. The only countries currently in membership with IPC not to have competed at a Summer Paralympic Games come from Africa (Cameroon, Congo, Gambia, Guinea-

Bissau, Liberia, Togo) and, perhaps rather surprisingly, Europe (Albania, Andorra). In nearly all cases their lack of participation is probably down to either a lack of finance or a lack of development of disability sport to a sufficient level. The picture for the Winter Paralympic Games, however, is very different with only 45 of the 161 nations (28 per cent) in membership with IPC having competed at a Winter Paralympic Games. The vast majority of these (69 per cent) come from Europe.

The major difference between the participation rates at the Summer and Winter Paralympic Games is likely to be geographical i.e. access to the necessary topographical (e.g. mountains) and climatic conditions (e.g. snow) needed for the regular practice of Winter sports. Those countries lacking these conditions would need to be able to afford to send athletes to train

Table 9.1 A comparison of participation by current IPC member nations at the Summer and Winter Paralympic Games up to and including Torino 2006 and Beijing 2008

	Africa	Americas	Asia	Europe	Oceania	Total
IPC membership	41	25	40	48	7	161
Summer Games	35	25	40	46	7	153
Winter Games	2	4	6	31	2	45

Table 9.2 Distribution of the medals at all Summer and Winter Paralympic Games by region up to and including Torino 2006 and Beijing 2008

Summer Games

Region	Gold	Silver	Bronze	Total	Total %
Africa	257	220	203	680	4
Americas	1314	1200	1233	3747	21
Asia	566	504	499	1569	9
Europe	3463	3479	3457	10399	59
Oceania	386	395	363	1144	7
IPA/IPP*	4	3	1	8	
Total	5990	5801	5756	17547	

Winter Games

Region	Gold	Silver	Bronze	Total	Total %
Africa	0	0	0	0	
Americas	118	128	102	348	15
Asia	14	26	25	65	3
Europe	646	619	626	1891	80
Oceania	25	10	15	50	2
IPA/IPP*	–	–	–	-	
Total	803	783	768	2354	

* IPA/IPP: Independent Paralympic athletes (2000)/independent Paralympic participants (1992)

in areas of the world where these conditions can be found, which makes participation in Winter sports for these nations a very expensive proposition indeed.

Table 9.2 shows the distribution of all medals by continental region for Summer and Winter Paralympic Games from their inception up to and including the Turin 2006 Winter Games and the Beijing 2008 Summer Games. This clearly highlights the European and North American dominance of both the Summer and Winter Games.

Given that the Paralympic Games were born in Great Britain and were heavily euro-centric in the early years and given that the world's major winter sports resorts are, on the whole, primarily in Europe and North America this historical dominance by European and North American nations is perhaps not surprising. Other nations, especially from Asia and Africa, joined the Paralympic Games later in their history, when competition for medals was greater, and so it is perhaps unsurprising that they fall behind in medal rankings. Table 9.3 shows the distribution of medals by continental region for the Turin 2006 Winter Games and the Beijing 2008 Summer Games. From the Beijing results it appears as though both Asia and Africa are gaining in strength and success at the Summer Paralympic Games as both almost doubled their respective share of the medals compared to their historical share of Summer Games medals. In truth, however, these results are down to just one nation from each continent. The host nation, China, won 64 per cent of all medals and 75 per cent of gold medals for the Asia region and South Africa won 28 per cent of all medals and 41 per cent of gold medals for the Africa region. If the medals for these two countries were removed and Table 9.3 was recalculated the results would be broadly in line

Table 9.3 Distribution of the medals at the Beijing 2008 Summer and Torino 2006 Winter Paralympic Games by region

Summer Games

Region	Gold	Silver	Bronze	Total	Total %
Africa	51	30	26	107	8
Americas	87	68	89	244	17
Asia	119	113	97	329	23
Europe	188	227	244	659	46
Oceania	28	33	31	92	6
Total	473	471	487	1431	

Winter Games

Region	Gold	Silver	Bronze	Total	Total %
Africa	0	0	0	0	
Americas	12	5	8	25	15
Asia	2	5	2	9	5
Europe	44	47	47	138	79
Oceania	0	1	1	2	1
Total	58	58	58	174	

with those in Table 9.2. This not only highlights the dangers of relying on statistics alone to examine and try and explain trends, but also possibly the advantages that richer nations may have in terms of preparing athletes and increasing their medal potential at a Paralympic Games.

Interestingly, the distribution of medals at the Turin 2006 Winter Paralympic Games and the overall historical distribution of Winter Games medals are almost identical, with perhaps Asian nations making very slight gains. This possibly underlines the importance of access to the necessary topographical, climatic and financial conditions outlined earlier in preparing athletes for the Winter Paralympic Games and is clearly underlined in Table 9.4 which shows the top ten overall medal winning nations at the Summer and Winter Paralympic Games. There are no countries from outside Europe and North America in the top ten Winter Games nations. Only Australia, who has competed since the first Summer Games in Rome, 1960 and China make it into the top ten Summer Games nations. China is an interesting case as they only began competing in the Paralympic Games in New York in 1984, but have risen to become the Summer Paralympic powerhouse nation

Table 9.4 The top ten overall medal winning nations at the Summer and Winter Paralympic Games

Summer Games

	Gold	Silver	Bronze	Total
USA	701	627	640	1968
Great Britain	529	507	496	1532
Germany*	469	467	444	1380
Canada	379	304	320	1003
France	330	323	311	964
Australia	327	350	315	992
Netherlands	250	216	185	651
Poland	241	229	188	658
China	236	188	134	558
Sweden	226	219	166	611

Winter Games

	Gold	Silver	Bronze	Total
Norway	133	98	78	309
Germany*	108	103	95	306
Austria	99	104	100	303
USA	92	92	64	248
Finland	75	47	59	181
Switzerland	48	53	48	149
France	46	40	47	133
Russia	43	43	29	115
Canada	26	36	38	100
Sweden	25	30	38	93

* These totals include medals won by the former Federal Republic of Germany (FRG) and the German Democratic Republic (DDR)

over the last two Summer Games. This will be discussed in more detail in the section of this chapter that looks at Asia in more detail.

Study activity

Andorra has competed at the last two Winter Paralympic Games, but has never competed at a Summer Paralympic Games. It is the only nation in Paralympic history to be in this situation. Find out what you can about Andorra and suggest possible reasons for this unique situation.

The remainder of this chapter will look in slightly more detail at each of the continental regions. Each section will start with a table showing the top three medal performing nations at the Summer and Winter Paralympic Games from that region. There will then be a short overview of any interesting or pertinent facts regarding the region and the Paralympic Games. Finally, each section will finish with 'snapshots' of nations within that region. The aim of these 'snapshots' is to introduce a variety of issues that may impact on participation in and performances at the Paralympic Games. These issues may be relevant nationally, regionally or globally. The nations chosen for these 'snapshots' are generally those where sufficient information was available to enable the writing of a sufficiently interesting and relevant 'snapshot'.

Africa

Table 9.5 Top three medal winning nations from the African region at the Summer and Winter Paralympic Games

Summer Games

	Gold	Silver	Bronze	Total
South Africa	102	76	73	251
Egypt	42	54	54	150
Tunisia	23	23	9	55

Winter Games

	Gold	Silver	Bronze	Total
	No Medallists			

In all a total of fifteen of the forty-one African nations currently in membership with IPC have won at least one medal of any colour at the Summer Paralympic Games. Only Uganda (1976, 1980) and South Africa (1998 onwards) from the African region have ever competed in a Winter Paralympic Games. Neither has ever won a medal.

Zimbabwe

Zimbabwe is one of eight countries in Southern Africa together with Angola, Botswana, Malawi, Mozambique, Namibia, South Africa, and Zambia. It has a total area of 390,759 square kilometres and a population of just over 13 million people (United Nations Statistics Division, 2006). Eighty per cent of the population lives in rural areas and 20 per cent in the cities. According to Mpofu and Harley (2002) the Government of Zimbabwe, in an Inter-Censual Demographic Survey (1997), established a total of 218,421 people with disabilities in the country (56 per cent males, 44 per cent females). Seventy-five per cent of people with disabilities lived in rural areas and 25 per cent in urban areas. Zimbabwe has competed at every Summer Paralympic Games since Arnhem, 1980 having previously competed as Rhodesia from 1960 until 1972. They have never competed at a Winter Paralympic Games.

Zimbabwe has previously been referred to as 'one of the most disability-accessible countries in Africa' (Devlieger, 1998, p. 26 in Mpofu and Harley, 2002) with greater availability of disability-friendly public transport policies, disability legislation, and the vocational training and employment opportunities of persons with disabilities compared to neighbouring countries. However, over the last decade there has been a well publicised economic collapse within the country. The eviction of more than 4,000 white farmers in the controversial land redistribution of 2000 has led to a sharp decline in agricultural exports, especially tobacco. Life expectancy at birth for males in Zimbabwe has dramatically declined since 1990 from 60 to 37, the lowest in the world. Life expectancy for females is even lower at 34 years. Concurrently, the infant mortality rate has climbed from 53 to 81 deaths per 1,000 live births in the same period. Currently, 1.8 million Zimbabweans live with HIV. Inflation rose from an annual rate of 32 per cent in 1998 to an official estimated high of 11,200,000 per cent in July 2008 and the central bank introduced a new 100 billion dollar note (CNN, 2008).

Under such stringent economic hardships it is usually the poor and the weak that suffer first and the hardest. People with disabilities, who generally live at or below the poverty line are usually amongst the groups to be hit hardest under such conditions. With the virtual collapse of the health service in Zimbabwe, people with disabilities are doubly hit as treatment and services they rely on slowly disappear. Yet despite this Zimbabwe still managed to send two athletes to the Beijing Paralympic Games (the same two they sent to the Athens Paralympic Games). One was Elliot Mujaji, who having qualified to race at the 1998 Commonwealth Games lost an arm in an electrical accident whilst working at the Shabanie Mine in 1999. He recovered to win Zimbabwe's first Paralympic Gold medal in Sydney, 2000 and repeated the feat in Athens four years later. However, according to Brickhill (2001) the government support Mujaji receives is very poor. He relies heavily on the generosity of individuals and companies including the mining company that has employed him both before and after his accident and who give him as much paid sporting leave as he needs and pay some of his travel expenses.

Kenya

The Republic of Kenya lies on the equator in East Africa. It is bordered by the Indian Ocean and by Ethiopia, Somalia, Tanzania, Uganda and Sudan. It covers an area of 580,367 square kilometres and has a population of just under 38 million people (United Nations Statistics Division, 2006). Data on the number of people with disabilities in Kenya is scarce, but according to Crawford (2004) a Kenyan Government survey conducted in 1989 found that roughly 2 per cent of the country's population had some kind of disability. Kenya first competed in the Summer Paralympic Games in Heidelberg in 1972 and, with the exception of 1976 where they participated in the Kenyan Olympic boycott, they have competed at every Summer Games since. They have never competed at a Winter Paralympic Games. In terms of medals they lie forty-sixth on the all-time Summer Paralympic medals table (1960–2008) with sixteen gold, fourteen silver and eleven bronze. In terms of Summer Olympic medals they lie thirty-sixth on the all-time medals table (1896–2008) with twenty-two gold, twenty-nine silver and twenty-four bronze. Interestingly, Kenya's very first Paralympic medal was won by Dr John Britton, who having won several medals for Great Britain at the 1968 Paralympic Games in Tel Aviv emigrated to Kenya and then won a gold medal in swimming in Heidelberg in 1972.

Crawford (2004) also cites a number of other telling statistics that arose from the Kenyan government survey. These include the following facts: first, roughly 81 per cent of people with disabilities' parents or guardians come from the poorest economic levels (pp.12–13), second, 91 per cent live in rural areas where access to facilities such as education, training and employment are very scarce (p.16) and third, in the 1980s 50 per cent of Kenyans with disabilities had no children, compared to the average Kenyan family of six or more children (p. 13). Crawford attributes this last fact to myths surrounding passing on 'bad blood' combined with perceptions that people with disabilities are 'asexual, unable to care for children, or are medically incapable' (Crawford, 2004, p. 13). This concept of 'bad blood', similar to the idea of karma described in the snapshot of Cambodia, plays a key part in impacting the way many people with disabilities are treated in Kenya compared to the non-disabled. However, non-disabled family members of people with disabilities may also be deemed to be tainted by the same curse, meaning whole families may be treated differently or even shunned. The overall result for people with disabilities and their families combined with the relative poverty and lack of opportunities to access services makes taking part in sport for the majority of Kenyans with a disability extremely difficult. Indeed as Crawford (2004, pp. 83–84) highlights inadequate nutrition for athletes with disabilities is a major problem in Kenya with several coaches cited as being fearful of pushing their athletes too hard for fear they had not even eaten that day.

The Americas

Table 9.6 Top three medal winning nations from the Americas region at the Summer and Winter Paralympic Games

Summer Games

	Gold	Silver	Bronze	Total
USA	701	627	640	1968
Canada	379	304	320	1003
Mexico	87	84	81	252

Winter Games

	Gold	Silver	Bronze	Total
USA	92	92	64	248
Canada	26	36	38	100
		No other medallists		

Nineteen of the twenty-five nations from the Americas region currently in membership with IPC have won at least one medal of any colour at the Summer Paralympic Games. Chile (2002, 2006) and Mexico (2006) are the only nations other than USA and Canada from the Americas region to have competed at a Winter Paralympic Games. Neither have won a medal.

The USA

The United States of America (USA) is the wealthiest country on earth. It covers 9,826,630 square kilometers and has a population of about 305 million people (United Nations Statistics Division, 2006) According to a Reuters Health (2008) report during 2004–2006, an estimated 20 per cent of US adults had some level of disability. The USA is one of only five nations to have competed at every Summer and Winter Paralympic Games. In terms of medal count up to and including the Beijing, 2008 Summer Games and the Turin 2006 Winter Games they are the most successful Summer Games nation and the fourth most successful Winter Games nation (see Table 9.4). This is broadly in line with their success at the Olympic Games where they are the most successful Summer Olympic nation and the second most successful Winter Olympic nation. With the exception of 1972 when they finished second to host nation, Germany, the USA topped the medal table at every Summer Paralympic Games from Tokyo, 1964 to Atlanta, 1996. However, since then they have finished fifth at Sydney, fourth at Athens and third at Beijing. In the Winter Games from Tignes, 1992 to Salt Lake City,

2002 they were never outside the top three and then in Turin 2006 they suddenly dropped to fifth.

Interestingly, this apparent decline in performance at the Paralympic Games by the USA has not been matched by any drop in performance at the Olympic Games, where the Winter Games team has actually got more successful over the last three Winter Games and they have topped the Summer Games medal table for three of the last four Games only losing out to host nation China in Beijing. There are many possible reasons for this apparent decline in performance over the last decade by the American Paralympic team including the increased entries and performance levels worldwide in disability sport. However, there have been several issues prevalent in the USA that have come to a head over the last decade that may have played a part in this decline. Since the Stevens Amendment to the Amateur Sports Act in 1998 (Hums *et al.*, 2003), which amongst other things was supposed to clarify the United States Olympic Committee's (USOC) responsibilities for Paralympic sport, there has been growing unrest amongst the American disability sports fraternity at what many see as discriminatory practices by USOC in the way it treats its non-disabled athletes vis-à-vis the athletes with disabilities it is responsible for. According to Byzek (1999) in the four years leading up to the Sydney Olympic and Paralympic Games the USOC budget for Olympians was around $370 million to cover such services as health insurance, training at the San Diego training facilities, direct support of athletes, and so on, none of which the Paralympic athletes were eligible for. The total budget for Paralympic sport for the same period was $7.6 million. For 2007 competitions, USOC distributed $1.85 million in performance bonuses, but none of it went to Paralympic athletes (Schwartz, 2008)

This led to a spate of lawsuits against USOC notably by Mark Shepherd, USOC's Director of Disabled Sport at the time, claiming that USOC discriminated against athletes with disabilities by providing separate and drastically inferior services and that these actions violated the Americans with Disabilities Act, the Rehabilitation Act and the Civil Rights Act (Hums *et al.*, 2003). This was followed in 2003 by a further lawsuit by three American Paralympians, Scot Hollenbeck, Tony Iniguez and Jacob Heilveil also claiming discrimination. In a New York Times article Alan Schwartz (2008) claims that the United States' performance at the Paralympics has decreased markedly over the last twenty years and was now on a par with countries with much smaller populations, which it had previously beaten easily. Schwartz cites Liz Nicholl, Great Britain's director of elite sport, who apparently stated that the manner in which the United States supported its disabled athletes was a top cause of the aforementioned decrease in performance and that she felt that the US was a nation that was 'choosing to under-perform'. Despite these legal challenges both the United States District Court and the United States Court of Appeals have ruled that USOC has the legal discretion to finance non-disabled athletes and athletes with disabilities differently and the Supreme Court has refused to hear an appeal. However the District Court judge who ruled against the Hollenbeck *et al.* lawsuit in 2006 wrote 'Do I decry a culture that relegates Paralympians to second-class status in the quantity and quality of benefits and support they receive from the USOC? Emphatically yes' (Schwartz, 2008).

In addition to problems with USOC, athletes with disabilities and their supporters in the United States also have to deal with another major issue – a complete refusal by the major television networks in the United States to give any live coverage whatsoever to the Paralympic Games, despite blanket coverage of the Olympic Games. For the last three or four Summer Paralympic Games interested viewers have had to content themselves with a one or two-hour documentary special put out several months after the Games had finished. This has led to many campaigns on platforms such as social networking sites like Facebook to get live coverage of the Paralympic Games on to the major networks and is possibly the reason why the biggest usage of the IPC internet site ParalympicSport.TV has been from American viewers during the last two Games in Turin, 2006 and Beijing, 2008 (see Chapter 6). However, on a positive note it should be pointed out that after twice finishing outside the top three in the Summer Games medal table in Sydney and Athens the United States did manage to climb back up to third place in Beijing, 2008.

Asia

Table 9.7 Top three medal winning nations from the Asian region at the Summer and Winter Paralympic Games

Summer Games

	Gold	Silver	Bronze	Total
China	236	188	134	558
South Korea	110	88	83	281
Japan	109	110	118	337

Winter Games

	Gold	Silver	Bronze	Total
Japan	14	24	25	63
Kazakhstan	0	1	0	1
South Korea	0	1	0	1

Of the forty nations currently in membership with IPC from the Asia region twenty-five have won at least one medal of any colour at the Summer Paralympic Games. China (2002, 2006), Iran (1998 onwards) and Mongolia (2006) are the only other nations from this region to have competed at the Winter Paralympic Games, but none has won a medal.

Cambodia

Cambodia is a country in South-East Asia covering just over 180,000 square kilometres and with a population, estimated in 2008, of just over 14 million (United Nations Statistics Division, 2006). Estimates for the number of disabled people in Cambodia vary widely ranging from 170,000 (NIS, 2003) to 1.4 million (ADB, 1999). The Disability Knowledge and Research Report (2005) on disability and poverty in Cambodia states that the major causes of disability in Cambodia are accidents, illness, war/conflict and landmines and other unexploded ordnance. Overarching all of these, the report claims that the major cause of all disability is poverty, with 36 per cent of the population living below the poverty line. According to the report:

> It is poor people who are usually the victims of mine and UXO accidents, as they are forced to live near and enter mine affected areas to collect food or firewood (International Campaign to Ban Landmines, 2004). They are also forced to use less safe methods of transport and to work in risky environments. In addition, their lack of access to basic health care means that simple infections, illnesses and injuries often result in permanent disability because they go untreated or are mistreated.
>
> (Disability Knowledge and Research, 2005, p. 6)

Cambodia has competed at the Summer Paralympic Games since Sydney 2000 when they entered a men's standing volleyball team. However, after Sydney standing volleyball was dropped from the programme. Since then they have sent one male and one female amputee track athlete to Athens and one male amputee track athlete to Beijing. Cambodia has never competed at a Paralympic Winter Games, nor have they ever won a Paralympic medal of any colour. Cambodia has the highest percentage of amputees in the world (Handicap-international, 2008) and so it is perhaps unsurprising that, thus far, all of their entries at the Paralympic Games have been amputees. Following nearly two decades of conflict, both internal and cross-border, some semblance of normality and regeneration began in the early to mid-1990s. The re-establishment of sport within Cambodian society has been via a mixture of government run sports structures and interventions by various charity based and non-governmental organisations such as Handicap-International (HI) and the Cambodian National Volleyball League (Disabled) (CNVLD), although, unlike CNVLD, HI have not been responsible for setting up any long term sports structure within the country. The CNVLD set up a Cambodian National Disabled Volleyball League in 1996 with just two teams in Phnom Penh that has grown into a sixteen team, two league competition. In 2007, Cambodia hosted the WOVD Standing Volleyball World Cup, the first ever team sports world cup event to held in the nation. In 2005 they added a Cambodian National Wheelchair Racing programme modelled on the club based volleyball structure. By 2008, all

CNVLD programmes were implemented through support from commercial sponsorship, which although helping to ensure the sustainability of their programmes also means they have barely scratched the surface of what could be achieved with adequate funding.

According to the CNVLD (official communication with author), since 1993 sport in Cambodia has been largely governed by Royalist political influences within the power sharing government that has led to a lack of investment in athletes and facilities as well as endemic corruption. The CNVLD claims that the nature of the patronage system, which largely defines the power structures of Cambodian society, has not assisted sports development due to individuals gaining positions of authority, which are then used to enrich the lives of themselves and their immediate family. This apparently led, in 2008, to CNVLD pulling their wheelchair racing team out of the ASEAN Games in Thailand due to the fact that the head of the National Paralympic Committee took a delegation that exceeded the number of athletes and which consisted of direct family members. A similar situation apparently occurred at the Beijing Games where the non-disabled team consisted of just four athletes and thirteen high-ranking officials leading to numerous media reports in which athletes complained about their lack of support.

One final issue raised by the CNVLD and worthy of mention is the fact that Cambodia is a Buddhist nation. The central precept of Buddhism revolves around 'karma' whereby actions in this life dictate the level of existence in the next. At a conceptual level, this often means that disability is seen as a punishment for bad actions committed in previous lives. Persons with a disability, especially in rural areas are, therefore, often hidden by their families who are afraid of their reputations in the wider community – specifically the very Asian idea of 'losing face'. This means that overcoming these fears of both the person with a disability and their family may at times make it even harder to persuade them to take part in sport, where the very cause of their fears (their disability) is even more visible to those around them.

Not only does this underline the important link between poverty and disability, but also the important role national and sports politics, and even religion, can play in either aiding or hindering progress in the development of a viable sports structure for people with disabilities. However, international sports politics can also have a major impact on developing nations. According to CNVLD, one of the biggest issues the organisation has faced is the exclusion of standing volleyball from the Paralympic Games programme which has apparently 'drawn sharp criticism from developing nations who feel that low-cost, participatory sports are being excluded in favour of sports only athletes in developed nations can afford to play.'

China

China has gone from a Paralympic also ran in 1984 to become the strongest Paralympic nation in the world by far at both the Athens, 2004 and Beijing, 2008 Paralympic Games. Table 9.8 shows the development of China's performance at every Summer Paralympic Games since it first began competing in 1984.

As can be seen from the table, China has improved its share of the medals at every Paralympic Games it has competed in (with the exception of 1992 when it sent a much smaller squad) even though the number of countries winning medals has almost doubled in the same period.

Under Mao strong and fit bodies were a pre-requisite for a strong and fit China. Sport and physical education were considered a vital component of nation building because the mother body, China itself, is considered to be made up of all of the bodies within it. Therefore, if they are strong and fit then China itself is also considered to be strong and fit to take on the world (Stone, 2001). MacClancey (1996) claims that sports may be used as a resource by which the powerful attempt to dominate others. The forgers of the Soviet state were well aware of its potential. To them, sport was a tool for socialising the population into the newly established system of values. Fan Hong *et al.* (2005) draw a similar conclusion about China when they state that the Chinese government uses sport as a window to show the world the new image of communism in the new era; as an ideology to unite Chinese people in a sporting patriotism as Marxist-Leninist and Maoist ideological beliefs begin to decay and as an opium to distract attention from severe social problems such as corruption and unemployment. They go on to claim that since the 1980s China's sport success has been regarded not only as evidence of ideological superiority and economic prosperity, but also the a totem of national revival. Attending the Olympics and other international competitions and performing well became the symbolic means of catching up with and even beating the western powers. 'Develop elite sport and make China a superpower in the world' became both a slogan and dream for the Chinese (Fan Hong *et al.*, 2005).

So where do the disabled, who account for between 60–100 million people in China, fit into this philosophy? According to Chi Jian (2005), Vice Chancellor of Beijing Sports University, attitudes to disabled people is one of the standards by which the progress of social civilisation is measured. He also claims that China has held sports competitions for the disabled since the 1950s. So is China's rise to superiority in Paralympic sport really a true reflection of the way people with disabilities are regarded and treated within Chinese society? Much has been made of the fact that Deng Pufang, the son of former Chinese Leader Deng Xioaping, and himself confined to a wheelchair, leads the Chinese Disabled Peoples Federation (CDPF). Many new laws have been passed aimed at improving the lives of disabled people and international recognition has been gained through the success of the

Table 9.8 China's Performances at the Summer Paralympic Games (1984–2008)

	Total team size	Men	Women	Position	Countries winning medals	Gold	Silver	Bronze	Total	% of all available medals
New York, 1984	24	18	6	23	38	2	12	8	22	1.3
Seoul, 1988	43	28	15	14	48	17	17	9	43	2.0
Barcelona, 1992	24	13	11	12	55	11	7	7	25	1.7
Atlanta, 1996	37	27	10	9	60	16	13	10	39	2.5
Sydney, 2000	87	54	33	6	68	34	22	17	73	4.4
Athens, 2004	203	111	92	1	75	63	46	32	141	9.0
Beijing, 2008	334	199	135	1	76	89	70	52	211	14.7

Chinese Paralympic team and the Disabled People's Arts Troupe that has toured the world. However, Stephen Hallett, a visually impaired reporter for the BBC who lives in Beijing and has a Chinese wife, states in a series of articles about life in China, that according to most of his disabled friends in China, the CDPF has become deeply corrupt, bureaucratic and self-serving. The hype of the Paralympics and the Disabled People's Art Troupe is quite unrepresentative of the tens of millions of people with disabilities who have seen little improvement in their lives (Hallett, 2006a). In a further article he quotes:

> China's disability organizations aren't there to serve disabled people Wang Yan told me the other day. They are primarily there to serve the government and make a good impression on foreigners.
>
> (Hallett, 2006b)

In the same article he relates the tale of a blind former local government official, Fu Yun, who went blind in her forties, taught herself Braille and offered her services to CDPF as a volunteer only to be told 'we don't have disabled people working here. What do you think a blind person like you can do?' (Hallett, 2006b).

Stone (2001) claims that under both Maoist body principles and Deng Xioaping's free-market economy, both have led to the alienation of the disabled – the former for their weakness and the latter for their non-productivity. She goes on to state that the propaganda surrounding disability sport has been another mechanism through which to shift the burden of disability away from the state and on to society in general and disabled people in particular. The government often holds up examples of courageous disabled, such as Paralympic champions, to encourage and possibly shame for not doing their part, other disabled into following suit. Unfortunately this appears to be without providing the means to do so, as is evident in the following comment from Wang Xinxian, the Vice Chairman of CDPF, who stated 'all of our disabled players are non-professional athletes and most do not have a stable job. They have to consider their family's economic situation when doing sports. Some excellent athletes have had to give up sports for financial reasons' (Tang, 2004).

Although the above is only a brief insight into China's possible motives for investing so heavily in Paralympic sport, it does appear from the evidence found that the success is not a true reflection of the way the disabled are treated and regarded within China. They appear to be taking similar approaches to those of the former Soviet Union and East Germany, only they are applying them to disability sport. Indeed Chi Jian (2005) stated that local sports associations for the disabled had set up files of adolescents and children in local hospitals, welfare institutions, elementary or middle schools and schools for disabled people. These measures were to help find talent as early as possible and as quickly as possible. It would appear then that China has a number of motivations behind its Paralympic success. On the one hand it wants to portray itself to the rest of the world as an economic power which looks after all of its people with equal care through its slogan 'develop elite sport and make China a superpower in the world.' On the other hand it wishes to distract the attention of its people from problems at home and to pass the issues surrounding disability on to society and disabled people in particular by holding up examples of Paralympic success to shame other disabled people into trying to make more of their lives without necessarily providing the means to help them. On a positive note, however, it cannot be denied that the Paralympic Games in Beijing were without doubt an extremely well run and highly successful Games. As Sir Philip Craven, President of the International Paralympic Committee, points out in his foreward to this book the success of these Games has created a new level of awareness of the Paralympic Games that can only be good news for the future of the Paralympic Movement.

Europe

Table 9.9 Top three medal winning nations from the European region at the Summer and Winter Paralympic Games

Summer Games

	Gold	Silver	Bronze	Total
Great Britain	529	507	496	1532
Germany*	469	467	444	1280
France	330	323	311	964

Winter Games

	Gold	Silver	Bronze	Total
Norway	133	98	78	309
Germany*	108	103	95	306
Austria	99	104	100	303

*These totals include medals won by the former Federal Republic of Germany (FRG) and the German Democratic Republic (DDR)

Forty-two out of forty-eight nations currently in membership with IPC from the European region have won at least one medal of any colour at the Summer Paralympic Games. A total of thirty-one nations currently in membership with IPC from the European region have competed at the Winter Paralympic Games out of a total of forty-five worldwide. This means that 69 per cent of nations that have competed at the Winter Paralympic Games are European.

Israel

Israel is located at the eastern end of the Mediterranean sea. It is bordered by Lebanon, Syria, Jordan and Egypt. It covers an area of just 20,770 to 22,072 square kilometres depending on whether you include or exclude the disputed territories of the Golan Heights and East Jerusalem and it has a population of just under 7.3 million people (United Nations Statistics Division, 2006). Israel has a relatively short history having only come into existence in May 1948. In the early years of its existence the majority of disabilities stemmed from two sources – conflicts with neighbouring countries, many of which are ongoing today, and a series of polio epidemics that caused a wave of infantile paralysis within the population. However, the way individuals with disabilities that result from these conflicts are viewed and treated in Israel compared with those with disabilities acquired from birth defects, disease and injuries is, even today, the cause of much dissatisfaction amongst the disabled population (Barnartt and Rotman, 2007). This disparity in treatment has a major impact on the opportunities each of these two groups have to take part in disability sport within Israel.

In much the same way as the Spinal Injuries Centre at Stoke Mandeville was set up to deal with spinally injured soldiers from World War II, following the War of Independence, which ended in 1949, the Zahal Disabled Veterans Organisation (ZDVO) was set up in order to assist the 6,000 soldiers disabled as a result of the conflict. In order to assist with the physical, psychological and social rehabilitation of these individuals the ZDVO set up special sports, rehabilitation and social centres, known as Beit Halochem centres, in Tel Aviv, Jerusalem and Haifa (Friends of Israel Disabled Veterans website, 2008). Beit Halochem centres, meaning 'House of the Warrior', offered these disabled veterans the opportunity to participate in programmes, including sport, that offer them opportunities to re-establish a regular routine, maintain physical fitness which prevents deterioration of their health and encourage them to renew social contacts that can be lost due to their hospitalisation and the isolation from the outside world that can occur for a variety of reasons (Zahal Disabled Veterans Organisation website, 2008). According to the Friends of Israel Disabled Veterans the number of ZDVO members has risen to 51,000 as a result of the ongoing conflicts in which Israel finds itself embroiled (Friends of Israel Disabled Veterans website, 2008).

For many years disabled war veterans have had the advantage of a system of benefits that means that they receive far better care and financial benefits than Israeli individuals injured as a result of birth defects or traumatic injuries or illness later in life. Indeed Dr Yaniv Poria, author of a study on the disabled in Israel stated that 'it is common among disabled people in Israel to say that it is better to become disabled during your army service than as a result of birth or an accident' (Israel21c website, 2008). Gal and Bar (2000) claim that disabled war veterans are more highly regarded within Israeli society than other disabled due to the fact that they received their disabilities in fighting in the name of Israel. Gal and Bar differentiate between the 'needed' and the 'needy' disabled individuals with the 'needed' disabled individuals having much higher status and far better care and remuneration than the 'needy' individuals, due to the sacrifices they made 'in the name of an array of social values'(Gal and Bar, 2005, p. 592). This greater care, access to services and financial remuneration has often meant that the majority of individuals achieving high level performances in disability sport within Israel have come from the ranks of the Israeli War Veterans. Indeed, Shved claimed in 2005 that about 70 per cent of the Israeli Paralympic team are Israeli Defence Force casualties. Shved claims this is probably due to 'the nature of their disability and the different attitude towards them in the public' (Shved, 2005, p. 3). Although civilian victims of terror attacks are now eligible for membership of ZDVO (Zahal Disabled Veterans Organisation website, 2008), the gap between the 'needed' and 'needy' disabled individuals is still to be bridged, not just in terms of sporting opportunity, but all aspects of social needs.

Norway

Norway is on the northern coast of Europe and is surrounded to the east by Finland, Russia and Sweden. It covers 385,252 square kilometres and has a population of just under 4.8 million people (United Nations Statistics Division, 2006). In 2005 around 10 per cent of the population of working age (16–66) was classified as being disabled (Statistics Norway, 2008). Norway is amongst the wealthiest countries in the world, due in the main to its oil production capabilities. However, much of Norway is dominated by mountainous or high terrain. This combination of geographical location and topographically challenging terrain, leading to climatic conditions that usually create an abundance of snow and ice appear to have played a major part in the sporting successes of Norway as a nation. Historically, Norway currently stands twenty-second in the overall combined Summer and Winter Olympic medal table and sixteenth in the overall combined Summer and Winter Paralympic medal table up to and including Beijing, 2008. However, for the overall Winter Olympic and Winter Paralympic medal tables it stands at the top of both tables some way ahead of its nearest rivals.

The first signs of skis being used are, apparently, on 4,500 to 5,000 year old rock drawings, such as those found at Rødøy in Norway. These drawings depict a man on skis holding a stick (Loveandpiste website, 2008). The people from the Telemark area of Norway have been largely credited with developing skiing into a sport, somewhere in the early 1700s (Speedski website, 2008) and Sondre Norheim, from Morgedal in Telemark, is known as the father of modern skiing for inventing the equipment and techniques that led to modern skiing as we know it today (Loveandpiste website, 2008). It is likely, therefore that the combination of historical development of skiing in Norway, the topographical and climatic conditions and the relative wealth of the country allowing easy access to all forms of skiing for the population have conspired to bring about the country's success in the Winter Olympic and Paralympic Games.

Oceania

Table 9.10 Top three medal winning nations from the Oceania region at the Summer and Winter Paralympic Games

Summer Games

	Gold	Silver	Bronze	Total
Australia	327	350	315	992
New Zealand	59	44	48	151
Papua New Guinea	0	1	0	1

Winter Games

	Gold	Silver	Bronze	Total
New Zealand	14	5	7	26
Australia	11	5	8	24
		No other medallists		

At the Beijing, 2008 Summer Paralympic Games, Papua New Guinea, became the first nation from the Oceania region, other than Australia or New Zealand, to win a Paralympic medal. Of the seven nations currently in membership with the IPC from the Oceania region only Australia and New Zealand have competed at the Winter Paralympic Games. However, it should be noted that the other five nations are all small island or small multi-island nations.

Fiji

Fiji lies in the heart of the Pacific Ocean midway between the Equator and the South Pole It consists of approximately 330 islands of which about one third are inhabited. These islands are spread over about 1.3 million square kilometres of the South Pacific Ocean. Fiji's total land area is only 18,333 square kilometers. There are two major islands – Viti Levu which is 10,429 square kilometers and Vanua Levu 5,556 square kilometers. The capital is Suva and it is one of the two cities in Fiji. The other city is Lautoka and both are located on the main island of Viti Levu (Fiji Government Website, 2008). The estimated population of Fiji in 2006 was just over 850,000 (United Nations Statistics Division, 2006). Nationwide statistics on disability in Fiji is not yet available. However, a number of persons with disabilities have been partly identified. In 1996, questions on disability were included in the national census in Fiji for the first time. In this census, nearly 12,000 persons were recorded as being disabled in some form. In the 1997 Fiji Poverty Survey, many persons with disabilities in Fiji were found to be poor and had limited formal education, employment opportunities, and services (Asia-Pacific Development Center on Disability, 2008).

Fiji first competed in the Paralympic Games as early as 1964 in Tokyo when Mr Nakatabula competed in the middle-weight weightlifting. However, it appears that Mr Nakatabula was a patient at Sydney Rehabilitation Hospital who was taken to Tokyo along with the Australian team rather than being sent from Fiji. Nakatabula had been injured in a mining accident whilst working for a Gold Mining Company in Fiji. Fiji first began competing regularly at the Summer Paralympic Games in Atlanta, 1996 and have sent a team, not exceeding four athletes, ever since. Fiji has never competed at a Winter Paralympic Games, nor has it ever won a Paralympic medal of any colour. There are numerous issues that impact on the recruitment and training of potential Paralympic athletes in Fiji, but two to be highlighted here are population dispersal and transportation. Taking into account that all the key sports facilities are on the main island of Viti Levu and that the population is dispersed between more than 100 islands over an area of more than 1 million square kilometres, travel for many potential athletes with a disability to coaching sessions and training facilities is extremely difficult if not impossible, especially on a regular basis. Availability of accessible boats, weather and sea conditions, the time necessary to travel between islands, the cost of that travel and many other factors all mount up to not only impact on the practicality of whether an individual can make the journey, but also whether they have the enthusiasm and drive to do the journey on a regular basis. According to Rob Regent of the Australian Sports Commission, who has been working closely with the Fiji Sports Association for the Disabled, from an original squad of twelve athletes that were in training for the Beijing, 2008 Paralympic Games only three were left by the time the Games came around and only one qualified. Regent cites as the most likely reason for this, the difficulties of transport in such a widely dispersed population (Regent, personal communication, 2008).

Jagdish Maharaj, team doctor for the Fijian Paralympic team in Beijing and founding President of the Fiji Sports Association for the Disabled, states that communities living away from the two main islands are very isolated. This not only makes travel to the main islands difficult, but is also part of the reason why accurate statistics regarding people with disabilities in Fiji are not available. This, in turn, makes identifying potential future Paralympians a major difficulty. Maharaj states that if a Fijian athlete with a disability really wants to succeed then they would have to move to the capital, Suva, but that they could probably only do this if they had good family support from someone already living there (Maharaj, personal communication, 2008). Regent echoed this view and gave as an example a young male amputee who was taken from his village, and his local support network, to the city. He apparently achieved very good results and qualified for Beijing in the high jump, but struggled greatly to adjust to life in the city. In the end he did not compete in Beijing (Regent, personal communication, 2008).

Australia

Australia is situated deep in the southern hemisphere and is an island country covering just over 7.41 million square kilometres with 34,218 kilometres of coastline. With a population of just under 21.5 million people it has one of the lowest population densities in the world at 2.6 people per square kilometre (United Nations Statistics Division, 2006). However, despite such a large land area the majority of Australia's population lives in one of the eight major cities that are sited at or near the coast. The 2003 Survey of Disability, Ageing and Carers found that 1 in 17 (5.9 per cent) of the population had a profound or severe level of disability and that one in five Australians (3,951,000 or 20 per cent) had some kind of disability (Australian Bureau of Statistics Website, 2008).

The federated state-territory system has both advantages and disadvantages for Australian sport. The advantage is that it is a relatively simple structural system where peak agencies such as the Australian Sports Commission are able to form agreements with state-territory departments and institutes for nationally driven initiatives. The disadvantage is that each state/territory has its own governmental system which may, or may not, be in alignment with the federal government. This federal system also impacts on national sports organisations and the relationships they have with their state/territory affiliates. These can conflict at any moment in time as national and state/territory priorities differ and change (Downs, 2008, personal communication).

Australia has actually been represented at every Summer and Winter Paralympic Games since they began. However, their only representative at the very first Winter Games in Örnsköldsvik, Sweden in 1976, Ron Finneran, was deemed ineligible to participate as his disability did not fit either the amputee or visual impairment classifications. Australia is also one of only two non-European or American region nations to make it into the overall top ten nations in terms of medal success at the Summer Paralympic Games.

There are many diverse opportunities for people with a disability to participate in sport across Australia. In recent years there has been a major shift towards enabling generic national sports organisations to take full responsibility for disability sport. The Australian Paralympic Committee (APC) and the Australian Sports Commission have focused efforts on generic sport through programmes such as the Paralympic Preparation Program (PPP) and Sports CONNECT. The PPP provides direct elite athlete support via the APC forming mainstream agreements with national sports organisations. Similarly, Sports CONNECT assists 25 national sports organisations to develop Disability Action Plans for their sport over a five year period. This has created an inclusive model where opportunities exist across the classic athlete pathway, from participation to competition to elite sport. Hence, athletes with disabilities are supported very well through the network of state and territory institutes and academies of sport and via state departments of sport and recreation (Downs, 2008, personal communication).

In order to try and overcome some of the issues raised by the sheer size of the country and the politics of the federated state-territory system in identifying new talent, the Australian Paralympic Committee introduced the 'Paralympic Search Program' with the aid of corporate sponsorship from Toyota. The aim of the programme is to identify people with physical disabilities or visual impairments who display the requisite athletic potential to one day make it to the Paralympic Games. This consists of a series of talent search days in each of the state-territories that are attended by coaches from each of the sports (APC Website, 2008). Between March 2005 and July 2008 more than 992 participants at these talent search days were screened, with eighty-nine identified as having potential for Beijing and a further 368 identified as longer term prospects. In the end twenty-seven athletes discovered by the programme qualified for Beijing and fourteen of those returned to Australia with a total of seventeen medals (APC Website, 2008).

Study activity

Cameroon, Congo, the Gambia, Guinea-Bissau, Liberia and Togo in Africa and Albania and Andorra in Europe are the only nations currently in membership with IPC who have never competed in a Summer Paralympic Games. Find out what you can about these nations and suggest reasons, other than finance, as to why they might be members of IPC, but never competed.

Conclusion

Hopefully this chapter has highlighted to the reader the variety and complexity of issues that can impact upon the participation and success of athletes with a disability around the world. The problems they face can be geographical, climatic, political, attitudinal, financial to name but a few. In certain cases, such as that highlighted in Norway, these issues can even have a positive impact on a country's success or otherwise at the Games. What is clear is that how these issues are managed or overcome will play a key role in the success or otherwise of nations and athletes aspiring to compete successfully in the Summer and Winter Paralympic Games.

Chapter review questions

1   What are some of the possible reasons for the overall differences in medal success at the Paralympic Games between the five continents?
2   What are the reasons why participation at the Winter Paralympic Games is dominated by European nations?
3   How well did your country do at the Beijing, 2008 Paralympic Games? What needs to change in your country to improve your country's chances of success at future Games?

Suggested further reading

Gilbert, K. and Schantz, O., 2008, *The Paralympic Games: Empowerment or Side Show?*, Meyer and Meyer, Maidenhead, UK.

10 The Special Olympics, intellectual disability and the Paralympic Games

Chapter aims

- Outline the development and aims of the Special Olympics Movement.
- Explain the differences between the Special Olympics and the Paralympic Games.
- Explain why athletes with an intellectual disability are currently banned from Paralympic competition and some of the ramifications of this ban.

There are still many individuals around the world who believe that the Special Olympics and the Paralympic Games are one and the same event. The aim of this chapter is, therefore, first, to explain the difference between the two movements. It will then go on to discuss the participation of athletes with an intellectual disability in the Paralympic Games and why they are currently banned from participation following the scandal that occurred with the Spanish Intellectually Disabled Basketball team at the Sydney 2000 Paralympic Games. The ramifications of this ban for both for the Paralympic Movement and for those athletes with an intellectual disability currently prevented from competing at the Paralympic Games will then be discussed.

The Special Olympics – the beginning.

The Special Olympics were started by Eunice Kennedy Shriver, a member of the politically and economically elite Kennedy family that dominated American politics in the 1960s and 1970s. As part of her work with the Joseph P. Kennedy Jr Foundation, set up in honour of the eldest son of Ambassador and Mrs Joseph P. Kennedy Sr who was killed in World War II, Eunice Kennedy Shriver visited many institutions built to house the numerous individuals with intellectual disabilities in the United States. Shocked by the terrible conditions and the total lack of educational or physical activity opportunities provided for these individuals she became determined that something had to be done. Herself an active sportswoman she was convinced that sport and physical activity could greatly enhance the lives of people with intellectual disabilities. In June 1962 she held a day camp, called Camp Shriver, for thirty-five boys and girls with intellectual disabilities at Timberlawn, her home in Rockville, Maryland in order to try out her theory using a variety of different sports and physical activities. Camp Shriver became an annual event and the Kennedy Foundation provided grants to various organisations to promote similar camps around the United States.

The Kennedy Foundation also began to promote workshops on the benefits of sports for everyone including individuals with an intellectual disability. This led to one attendee at a workshop from Chicago, Anne Burke, doing some work for the Chicago Parks Department on how they could do more for individuals with an intellectual disability. This eventually led to them working with the Kennedy Foundation to put on the First Special Olympics International Games in July 1968. Since that first Games the Special Olympics have developed into a worldwide organisation of over 2 million registered athletes from over 170 countries. The first Winter Games were introduced in Steamboat Springs, Colorado in 1977 and the first Games to be held outside the USA were the Winter Games held in Salzburg and Schladming in Austria in 1993. The Summer Games were first held outside the USA in 2003 when they were held in Dublin, Ireland. Table 10.1 shows how the main Special Olympics Summer and Winter Games have developed since they were first

Table 10.1 The development of the Summer and Winter Special Olympics Games

Year	Location	No. of countries	No. of athletes	No. of sports (inc. demo events)
1968	Chicago, USA	2	1000	3
1970	Chicago, USA	4	2000	NA
1972	Los Angeles, USA	8	2500	NA
1975	Michigan, USA	17	4000	NA
1977	**Colorado, USA**	5	525	2
1979	Brockport, USA	20	3500	NA
1981	**Vermont, USA**	11	700	2
1983	Baton Rouge, USA	50	4300	NA
1985	**Utah, USA**	14	900	2
1987	Indiana, USA	73	4700	NA
1989	**Nevada & California, USA**	18	1055	**NA**
1991	Minnesota, USA	104	5700	NA
1993	**Salzburg & Schladming, Austria**	60	1550	5
1995	Connecticut, USA	143	7000	21
1997	**Ontario, Canada**	73	2000	5
1999	North Carolina, USA	150	7000+	19
2001	**Alaska, USA**	70	1800	7
2003	Dublin, Ireland	150	6500+	21
2005	**Nagano, Japan**	84	1800+	7
2007	Shanghai, China	164	7500	25

Bold = Winter Games. NA = Information not available

introduced in 1968. As with the Paralympic Games, historical data for these Games is at best patchy and so the table is not complete.

Special Olympics – the name

Given the discussion in Chapter 2 regarding the use of Olympic terminology by the Paralympic movement and the reaction of the International Olympic Committee to this usage, some readers might be wondering why the Special Olympics movement gets away with it. Information on this issue is sketchy and hard to find, but letters in the IOC archive from the 1970s indicate that usage of Olympic terminology by the Special Olympics movement at that time was a very contentious issue. In a letter from Douglas F. Roby, former President of the United States Olympic Committee to the then IOC President Lord Killanin dated 28 December, 1974, Roby claims the issue began in around 1966 when 'a trap' was apparently set for the former IOC President Avery Brundage regarding the Special Olympics that led to him giving his endorsement to their use of the word 'Olympics' at their inaugural Games in Chicago. Roby apparently obtained verbal agreement from the Kennedys in both 1966 and 1967 that they would stop using the term Olympics. However, it appears that Roby's successors had a change of heart and in a letter from F. Don Miller of USOC to Madame Berlioux at the IOC dated 20 December, 1978 Miller admits that the USOC Executive Board did grant the Special Olympics Organisation the right to use the term 'Special Olympics', but only within the United States' borders. According to the Special Olympics website this occurred in December 1971. Madame Berlioux responded to Miller in the following January stating that all NOCs would be contacted and instructed to stop the use of the word 'Olympics' on their territory and that the Special Olympics Organisation would be requested to replace the term 'Olympics' in their title with another appropriate term. As history has shown this never happened and in February 1988 the Special Olympics organisation was officially recognised by the IOC and is the only non-Olympic organisation with official permission to use the term 'Olympics' in its title. How this came about can only be a matter for conjecture at present. However, it is likely that a combination of the influential political and economic power of the Kennedys combined with the massively influential role the Los Angeles Olympic Games and the part corporate sponsorship had in saving the Olympic movement from financial ruin, played key roles in this. The financial and political influence of the United States Olympic Committee within the Olympic movement, as the American TV companies and other major corporate sponsors have become ever greater contributors to the Olympic coffers, may also have played a part in this decision.

Special Olympics – their aim

The Special Olympics organisation has seven regional offices around the world and encompasses more than 170 countries. It claims to have more than 700,000 volunteers and 500,000 officials organising over 25,000 competitions within more than 200 Special Olympic programmes around the world each year. It defines itself as follows:

Mission

The mission of the Special Olympics is to provide year-round sports training and athletic competition in a variety of Olympic-type sports for children and adults with intellectual disabilities, giving them continuing opportunities to develop physical fitness, demonstrate courage, experience joy and participate in a sharing of gifts, skills and friendship with their families, other Special Olympics athletes and the community.

Vision

The Special Olympics movement will transform communities by inspiring people throughout the world to open their minds, accept and include people with intellectual disabilities and thereby celebrate the similarities common to all people.

Eligibility

Special Olympics athletes must be at least eight years old and identified by an agency or professional as having one of the following conditions: intellectual disabilities, cognitive delays as measured by formal assessment, or significant learning or vocational problems due to cognitive delay that require, or have required, specially designed instruction.

Competition

Special Olympics athletes are divided into competition divisions based upon their ability, age and sex. Competition divisions are structured so that athletes compete against other athletes of similar ability in equitable divisions. A fair and equitable division is one in which all participants, based on performance records, have a reasonable chance to excel. This definition also applies to team competition. (Special Olympics International Website, 2008).

The Special Olympics and the Paralympic Games – the differences

The Special Olympics organisation and the International Paralympic Committee are both sporting organisations for people with disabilities that are recognised by the International Olympic Committee. They both hold Summer and Winter Games on a four yearly cycle. However, the Paralympic Games are held in conjunction with the Olympic Games in the same host city and using the same sporting facilities and starting two to three weeks after the closing ceremony for the Olympic Games. The Special Olympic Winter Games are held in the year following the Olympic and Paralympic Summer Games and the Special Olympic Summer Games are held in the year following the Olympic and Paralympic Winter Games. The principal differences between the Special Olympic and Paralympic movements lie in the levels of sporting ability of the participating athletes as well as the actual disability of the athletes.

Ability level

The Special Olympics involves athletes from all ability levels with participation from the full range of intellectual disability. In order to assure fair competition, Special Olympics athletes are placed in divisions with other athletes of similar ability. Each division has a final allowing all athletes a fair opportunity to compete with a chance to win. In addition, although the first three in each final receive a medal, every other competitor receives a participation ribbon. This system is designed to challenge each athlete to do his or her best while providing a meaningful and enjoyable experience.

The Paralympic Games involves athletes from six disability groups who compete only at the elite sports level. As in mainstream sports competition, athletes who do not meet qualifying standards may not compete and others who are competing may lose in preliminary play. The mainstream philosophy of sport is applied that facilitates competition to determine the best individual athlete or team.

Disability criteria

The Special Olympics competition is, first and foremost, for individuals who have an intellectual disability. They may also have additional physical or sensory disabilities, but in order to qualify to take part they must have an intellectual disability.

In order to participate in the Paralympic Games individuals must come from a one of six disability groups as described in Chapter 1. Although these six groups do include one for intellectual disabilities, athletes with intellectual disabilities who aspire to compete at the Paralympic Games are not represented by the Special Olympics organisation.

Study activity

Why do you think so many people think the Special Olympics and the Paralympic Games are the same event? What could be done to improve understanding and appreciation of the two events by the general public?

The International Sports Federation for People with an Intellectual Disability.

The International Sports Federation for People with an Intellectual Disability (INAS-FID) was formed in 1986 with the aim to create a platform for athletes with an intellectual disability who wish to perform their sport competitively, in open competition (as at the Olympics) and according to the rules of the mainstream International Sports Federations. The difference in the sporting ethos and philosophy between INAS-FID and the Special Olympics organisation is exactly the same as the difference between those of the Paralympic movement and the Special Olympics organisation with regard to ability level. However, athletes represented by INAS-FID at the Paralympic Games are currently banned from competition at both the Paralympic Games and IPC World and regional championships.

Intellectually disabled athletes at the Paralympic Games

The International Association of Sports for Persons with a Mental Handicap, which later became the International Sports Federation for People with an Intellectual Disability (INAS-FID), were accepted into membership of the International Co-ordinating Committee at their tenth meeting held in Gothenburg in 1986. Although events for athletes with an intellectual disability were added to the programme for the Winter Games in Tignes, 1992 it was decided that a separate summer Games, sanctioned by ICC, would be held in Madrid immediately after the Games in Barcelona, 1992 as part of their gradual inclusion into the overall Paralympic framework. A total of seventy-five nations from all five continents gathered in Madrid for the Games to compete in sixty-eight events spread over five sports. However, in Atlanta four years later when intellectually disabled athletes first competed in the Summer Paralympic Games proper there were only fifty-six athletes competing in athletics and swimming. This grew four years later in Sydney to 244 athletes competing in athletics, swimming, table tennis and basketball. All seemed to have gone well and participation of athletes with intellectual disabilities at the Paralympic Games appeared set to become a regular feature of the Games. Then something happened that was to rock the world of Paralympic and disability sport for many years to come.

The Sydney 2000 Paralympic Games eligibility scandal

On 21 October 2000 the Spanish intellectually disabled basketball team won the gold medal at the Sydney Paralympic Games beating Russia 87–63 in the final. This victory capped Spain's best ever performance at a Summer Paralympic Games winning 107 medals and finishing third in the medal table. However, triumph was to turn into disaster in late November when Carlos Ribagorda, a member of the gold medal winning basketball team and also a journalist with a Madrid-based business magazine, *Capital*, wrote an article chronicling long-term and widespread fraud and cheating within intellectually disabled sport in Spain. The pinnacle of his revelations was that ten of the twelve gold medal winning Spanish basketball players actually had no intellectual disability at all and had been deliberately recruited to increase the strength of the team in order to win medals and thus guarantee future funding. It also turned out that this was not a new occurrence, but had been going on for a number of years. It later transpired that four members of the Spanish intellectually disabled basketball team that had won the gold medal at the World Championships in Brazil also had no disability. The potential cheating was apparently not restricted to the sport of basketball either. One member of Spain's intellectually disabled track and field team, two swimmers and one table tennis player were suspected of not having a disability and went on to win medals.

At the centre of the growing storm was Fernando Vicente Martin, a former Madrid councillor who held numerous prominent positions in the world of disability sport. The father of a disabled daughter, he was an International Paralympic Committee Executive Board member, Vice-President of the Spanish Paralympic Committee, President of INAS-FID and President of the Spanish Sports Federation for the Intellectually Disabled (FEDDI). He was also founder and President of the National Association of Special Sports (ANDE), a charitable body for the intellectually disabled, which received generous state subsidies and was a major sponsor of the Madrid Paralympic Games for the Intellectually Disabled in 1992. Initially Vicente Martin denied any wrongdoing and claimed that all of the Spanish athletes were intellectually disabled, albeit many of them were very near the upper limits of the qualification criteria (maximum IQ of 75). According to Nash (2001) in an article in the UK newspaper, *The Independent* Martin initially denounced Ribagorda's article as the lies of a 'handicapped person who had gone mad'. The Spanish Paralympic Committee launched a full investigation in November 2000 and concluded not only that fraud had been committed in Sydney, but that Fernando Vicente Martin was the man responsible for the events that had occurred. In January, the Spanish Paralympic Committee expelled him and in February IPC suspended him and he resigned as President of INAS-FID.

As a result of the Spanish Paralympic Committee's findings, the International Paralympic Committee set up a commission of investigation in December 2000 to examine the allegations consisting of Andre Noel Chaker, a lawyer specialising in sports legislation, Dr Donald Royer of the IPC Legal Committee, Dr Lutz Worms, a specialist in sports medicine and Thomas Reinecke, IPC Chief Operating Officer. In January the Commission requested specific information for investigative purposes from INAS-FID including the INAS-FID registration cards for the 244 athletes who had participated in Sydney. In the end, according to issue 1 of *The Paralympian* (2001) the INAS-FID Secretariat forwarded 230 of the 244 registration cards. Fourteen cards were, therefore, missing and it later transpired that eleven cards provided were for athletes not accredited to compete in Sydney. These were excluded from the investigation. After careful scrutiny of the remaining 219 cards it was found that 157 (72 per cent) were found to be invalid in that one or more of the primary requirements was found to be incomplete or missing. The commission concluded that the eligibility verification of the forms at both national and international level had been seriously mismanaged and administered. To make matters worse it was found that 94 of the 132 possible medals for intellectually disabled events at the Sydney Games were awarded to athletes amongst the 157 cards deemed to be invalid. However, it should be pointed out that just because a card had been deemed invalid it did not automatically bring into question the athlete's eligibility.

Based upon these findings, on 29 January, 2001, the IPC Management Committee suspended INAS-FID, its President Fernando Vicente Martin and all athletes with an intellectual disability from all IPC activities. This decision was later upheld and endorsed at the IPC Executive Committee held in Salt Lake City on 9 March, 2001, where they approved five resolutions relating to the case:

I The IPC IC findings have proven beyond doubt that the process of assessment, verification and certification of intellectually disabled athletes was not properly carried out, supervised or audited. The IPC determined that the President and Technical Officer of INAS-FID, Mr. Fernando Martín Vicente and Mr. Felipe Gutiérrez García respectively, are primarily responsible for this serious violation. Consequently, it was decided that both be expelled from IPC with immediate effect.

II IPC demanded that the membership of INAS-FID review their eligibility criteria and process and implement a new mechanism following the recommendation of the IPC IC, which clearly defines the eligibility process, qualification and accreditation of assessors and standard documentation to the full satisfaction of IPC.

III IPC requests the National Paralympic Committees whose athletes submitted inaccurate or invalid documentation at the XI Paralympic Summer Games Sydney 2000 to review the status of their athletes by an independent investigation committee similar to that conducted by the Spanish Paralympic Committee, and to produce a findings report for the IPC IC within the next three (3) months, but no later than May 31, 2001.

All medals won by athletes who do not meet the international eligibility standards should be returned to IPC via the respective National Paralympic Committee.

IV IPC urges INAS-FID to admit their responsibility and accountability with regard to the current violations, and to rectify their policy and leadership at the upcoming General Assembly scheduled for April 2001, including the expulsion from their executive positions on the INAS-FID Executive Committee, members who voted in favor of the motion of confidence for Mr. Fernando Martin Vicente at the last INAS-FID Executive Committee meeting.

V Until and unless INAS-FID has resolved the above issues to the satisfaction of the IPC Executive Committee, the membership of INAS-FID will remain suspended indefinitely. INAS-FID may produce their new policy, and results of their investigation, to IPC at any time for consideration.

However, and as proof of respect to athletes with an intellectual disability, according to the definitions provided by the World Health Organisation and the American Association of Mental Retardation, the IPC Executive Committee accepts that competitions and events sanctioned by the IPC and involving athletes with an intellectual disability may continue to be planned and organised, including the VIII Paralympic Winter Games Salt Lake City 2002. Intellectually disabled athletes may obtain provisional recognition from IPC, if their eligibility is duly proven and verified by a new eligibility committee appointed by INAS-FID and IPC.

(The Paralympian, 2001/1, p. 3)

By late 2002 IPC and INAS-FID were still working together and making some progress towards the establishment of a new, more robust, eligibility system that encompassed stringent verification procedures. However, both sides agreed that the new system still did not meet the necessary criteria. Unfortunately, by early to mid-2003 it was decided that the new system was still not reliable enough and events for athletes with an intellectual disability were removed from the programme for Athens 2004. This situation remained the same some five years later. Athletes with an intellectual disability did not appear at the Beijing, 2008 Paralympic Games. However, at a joint meeting of a working group of members from both IPC and INAS-FID held during the Games in Beijing it appears that significant progress was made leading to a very positive sounding press release being issued. It laid out the outline of the new classification and testing system for athletes with an intellectual disability, which is to be piloted in early 2009 and ended with the statement

'It is envisaged that the inclusion of athletes with an intellectual disability in future Paralympic Games, beginning with London 2012, will be formally ratified by the IPC General Assembly in November 2009' (IPC Website, 2009h).

Study activity

Do you think banning athletes with an intellectual disability after the Sydney scandal was the right decision? What would you have done in this situation?

Fighting the ban and its impacts in the UK

If successful, the work of the IPC/INAS-FID working group will bring to an end almost a decade of struggle by athletes with intellectual disabilities and the organisations that represent them to be re-included in the Games. The impact of the ban on athletes with an intellectual disability and the organisations that represent them following the IPC ban was far reaching. Funding ceased to both the representative organisations and the athletes themselves, meaning that athletes had to fund themselves if they wished to continue representing Britain in international competition. Many simply could not afford to do so. According to the UK Sports Association for People with Learning Disability (UKSA) who represent British athletes 'UK athletes have been ejected, completely excluded or limited from competing and accessing various sporting competitions and schemes across the UK including the UK School Games' (UKSA News Release, 2008). UKSA claims that it has been leading a campaign, since the ban on athletes with an intellectual disability following the Sydney Games, working with its member organisations, the British Paralympic Association, RADAR, MENCAP, the Equality and Human Rights Commission (EHRC) and other organisations to get the ban overturned. On a national level, in co-operation with the EHRC, UKSA have been successful in having the ban removed on children with learning disabilities taking part in the UK School Games, which were set up by the Youth Sport Trust in 2006 to foster potential Olympic and Paralympic competitors. In future Games they will be allowed to compete in athletics, swimming and table tennis events. In response to the above mentioned press release regarding the possible re-inclusion of athletes with intellectual disabilities in the London 2012 Paralympic Games, UKSA still considered the statement to be 'disappointing after eight years of discussion' and called upon 'the Prime Minister, the London 2012 Organising Committee, the Secretary of State and the Mayor of London, to declare unequivocally that athletes with intellectual disability must be included in the Paralympics in London 2012' (UKSA, 2008). In an earlier news release EHRC stated that if persuasion failed it would not hesitate to use its legal powers to challenge what it considers unlawful discrimination against athletes with intellectual disabilities wishing to pursue their sport at the very highest levels in London 2012 (EHRC News Release, 2008).

Conclusion

Hopefully it is clear from this chapter that the Special Olympics and the Paralympic Movements are two completely separate, but equally valid, organisations with very different aims and serving two very different groups of clientele by similar means, but different methods. It should also be clear that even amongst the intellectually disabled sporting community there are those who wish to go down the Special Olympic route to meet their sporting needs and those who wish to compete in the Paralympic Games. The latter have their own organisation, which is again separate from the Special Olympics and which is part of the Paralympic family. The participation of intellectually disabled athletes within the Paralympic Games will hopefully have been settled by the time of the next Games in London in 2012.

Chapter review questions

1 What are the Special Olympics?
2 What are the differences between the Special Olympics and the Paralympic Games?
3 What are the possible reasons why the Special Olympics were allowed to continue using Olympic terminology when the Paralympic Movement was not?
4 Do you think it is right that athletes with an intellectual disability were banned from the Paralympic Games following what happened in Sydney? Give reasons for your answer.

Suggested further reading

Bueno, A., 1994, *Special Olympics: The First 25 Years, Foghorn Press*, San Francisco, USA.
Jobling, A., Jobling, I., and Fitzgerald, H., 2008, The Inclusion and Exclusion of Athletes with an Intellectual Disability in Cashman, R. and Darcy, S. (eds), *Benchmark Games: The Sydney 2000 Paralympic Games*, Walla Walla Press, Petersham, NSW, pp. 201–15.

Bibliography

Abberley, P., Disabled people and 'normality', in Swain, J., Finkelstein, V., French, S. and Oliver, M. (eds), 1993, *Disabling Barriers – Enabling Environments, Open University*, Milton Keynes, pp. 107–15.

Addelson, K.P., 1983, The Man of Professional Wisdom, in Harding, S. and Hintikka, M.B., 1983, *Discovering Reality*, Reidel, Boston, pp. 165–186.

Anderson, J., 2003, Turned in Tax Payers: Paraplegia, Rehabilitation and Sport at Stoke Mandeville, 1944–56, *Journal of Contemporary History*, Vol. 38 (3), pp. 461–75.

Asia-Pacific Developemnt Center on Disability website (http://www.apcdproject.org/countryprofile/fiji/fiji_org.html) accessed 15 October 2008.

Asian Development Bank (ADB), 1999, *Identifying Disability Issues Related to Poverty Reduction: Cambodia Country Study*, ADB, Phnom Penh.

Australian Bureau of Statistics Website, 2008, *Disability, Ageing and Carers: Summary of Findings, Australia, 2003* (http://www.abs.gov.au/Ausstats/abs@.nsf/e8ae5488b598839cca25682000131612/768ee722e31f6315ca256e8b007f3055!OpenDocument) accessed 15 October 2008.

Auxter, D., Pyfer, J., and Huettig, C., 1993, *Principles and Methods of Adapted Physical Education and Recreation*, Mosby, London.

Barnartt, S. and Rotman, R., 2007, *Disability Policies and Protests in Israel* (http://www.allacademic.com/meta/p_mla_apa_research_citation/1/8/4/1/0/p184101_index.html) accessed 27 October 2008.

Barnes, C., 1990, *'Cabbage Syndrome': The Social Construction of Dependence*, The Falmer Press, London.

Barnes, C., 1991, *Disabled People in Britain and Discrimination*, Hurst and Co, London.

Barnes, C., 1992, Qualitative Research: valuable or irrelevant?, *Disability, Handicap and Society*, Vol. 7 (2), 1992, pp. 115–24.

Barnes, C., 1994, *Disabled People in Britain and Discrimination* (2nd edn), Hurst and Co, London.

Barton, L., 1993, Disability, Empowerment and Physical Education, in Evans, J. (ed.), 1993, *Equality, Education and Physical Education*, The Falmer Press, London, pp. 43–54.

Bazylewicz, W, 1998, *Disability Sport: International Sports Organisation for the Disabled*, on Michigan State University website (http://ed-web3.educ.msu.edu/KIN866/isod.htm) accessed 15/2/99.

Birkenbach, J.,1990, *Physical Disability and Social Policy*, University of Toronto Press, Toronto.

BOCOG, 2008, Guidelines to Classification, BOGOG, Beijing; China, p.1.

Brandmeyer, G.A. and McBee, G.F., 1986, Social Status and Athletic Competition for the Disabled Athletes: The Case of Wheelchair Road-Racing, in Sherrill, C. (ed.), 1986, *Sport and Disabled Athletes*, Champaign, Il., Human Kinetics, pp. 181–7.

Brickhill, J., 2001, *Poor Support for Zimbabwe Star*, (http://news.bbc.co.uk/1/hi/world/africa/1375611.stm) accessed 20 October 2008.

Brittain, I., 2002, Elite Athletes with Disabilities: Problems and Possibilities, Unpublished PhD thesis. Buckinghamshire Chilterns University College, UK.

Brittain, I., 2004a, Perceptions of Disability and Their Impact Upon Involvement in Sport for People with Disabilities at All Levels, *Journal of Sport and Social Issues*, Vol. 28(4), pp. 429–52.

Brittain, I., 2004b, The Role of Schools in Constructing Self-perceptions Regarding Sport and Physical Education in Relation to People with Disabilities, *Sport, Education and Society*, Vol. 9(1), 75–94.

Brittain, I., 2008, *Studying (Able-Bodied?) Sports Development: Researching, Teaching and Writing in the Field*, Brunel University, UK, 25–26 April.

Brittain, I. and Wolff, E.,2007, Why Language Matters, Paper presented at the North American Society for Sociology of Sport Conference, Pittsburgh, Illinois, 31 October–3 November.

Broadcasting Standards Commission, 1999, Monitoring Report 7, BSC, London.

Brown, H. and Smith, H., 1989, Whose 'Ordinary Life' Is It Anyway?, *Disability, Handicap and Society*, 1989, Vol. 4(2), pp. 104–19.

Burr, V., 1995, *An Introduction to Social Construction*, Routledge, London.

Byzek, J., 1999, Bad Sports: US Olympic Committee thumbs nose at Paralympics (http://www.raggededgemagazine.com/0999/a0999cov.htm) accessed 28 November 2008.

Cashman, R. and Tremblay, D., 2008, Media, in Cashman, R. and Darcy, S. (eds), *Benchmark Games: The Sydney 2000 Paralympic Games*, Walla Walla Press, Sydney, pp. 99–122.

Cavet, J., Leisure and Friendship, in Robinson, C. and Stalker, K. (eds), 1998, *Growing Up with Disability*, Jessica Kingsley Publishers, London, pp. 97–110.

CBC Sports, 2008, *Pistorius Falls Short in Last-chance Run*, (http://www.cbc.ca/news/story/2008/07/16/pistorius-lucerne.html) accessed 9 December 2008.

Chambers Encyclopedic English Dictionary, 1994, Larousse PLC, Edinburgh, Scotland.

Chi Jian, 2005, The Development of Sports for the Disabled in China, Paper presented at the IV International Forum on Elite Sport, Montreal, Canada, July 26–28, 2005.

CNN Website, 2008, *Zimbabwe Inflation hits 11,200,000 Percent*, (http://edition.cnn.com/2008/BUSINESS/08/19/zimbabwe.inflation/index.html) accessed 20 October 2008.

The Cord, 1960, The 1960 International Stoke Mandeville Games for the Paralysed in Rome, 18–25 September, Special Edition, p. 14.

The Cord, 1949, Stoke Mandeville Calling, 2(4), pp. 34–5.

Craven, Sir P., 2006, *Paralympic Athletes Inspiring and Exciting the World*, presentation at the XIXth British National Olympic Academy, Greenwich, UK on 29 April, 2006.

Crawford, C., 1989, A view from the sidelines: disability, poverty and recreation in Canada, *Journal of Leisurability*, Vol. 16 (2), pp. 3–9.

Crawford, J., 2004, Constraints of Elite Athletes with Disabilities in Kenya, Unpublished Masters Thesis, University of Illinois at Urbana-Champaign, USA.

Cumberbatch, G. and Negrine, R., 1992, *Images of Disability on Television*, Routledge, London.

Darke, P. 1998, Understanding cinematic representation of disability, in Shakespeare, T. (ed.), *The Disability Reader: Social Science Perspectives*, Continuum, London p. 181–97.

Davis, L.J., 1997, Constructing Normalcy: The Bell Curve, the Novel, and the Invention of the Disabled Body in the Nineteenth Century, in Davis, L.J.(ed.), 1997, *The Disabilities Studies Reader*, Routledge, London, pp. 9–28.

DePauw, K.P., 1997, The (In)Visibility of DisAbility: Cultural Contexts and "Sporting Bodies" *Quest*, Nov. 1997, Vol. 49 (4), pp. 416–30.

DePauw, K.P., 2000, Social-Cultural Context of Disability: Implications for Scientific Inquiry and Professional Preparation, *Quest*, Vol. 52, pp. 358–68.

DePauw, K.P. and Gavron, S.J., 1995, *Disability and Sport*, Human Kinetics, Champaign, IL.

Devine, M.A., Inclusive Leisure Services and Research: A Consideration of the Use of Social Construction Theory, *Journal of Leisurability*, Spring 1997,Vol. 24(2), pp. 3–11.

Devlieger, P.J., 1998, Vocational rehabilitation in Zimbabwe: A Socio-Historical Analysis, *Journal of Vocational Rehabilitation*, Vol. 11, pp. 21–31.

Disability Daily, Exploding the Myths, Jan, 1998, in Donnellan, C. (ed.), 1998, *Issues: Disabilities*, Vol. 17, Independence, Cambridge, UK.

Disability Knowledge and Research, 2005, *Poverty Reduction and Development in Cambodia: Enabling Disabled People to Play a Role* (http://www.disabilitykar.net/docs/cambodia%20.doc) accessed 15 October 2008.

Donnellan, C. (ed.), 1998, *Issues: Disabilities*, Vol. 17, Independence, Cambridge, UK.

Downs, 2008; Personal Communication. Email from Peter Downs dated 29 May 2008.

Drake, R.F., 1999, *Understanding Disability Politics*, Macmillan, London.

Dunn, J.M. and Sherrill, C., 1996, Movement and Its Implication for Individuals with Disabilities, *Quest*, Aug. 1996, Vol. 48, 3, pp. 378–91.

Dyer, 2007; Personal Communication. Email from Bruce Dyer, 11 October 2007.

Fan Hong, Ping Wu and Huan Xiong, 2005, Beijing Ambitions: An Analysis of the Chinese Elite Sports System and its Olympic Strategy for the 2008 Olympic Games, *The International Journal of the History of Sport*, Vol. 22(4), pp. 510–29.

Felske, A.W., 1994, Knowing about Knowing: Margin Notes on Disability Research, in Rioux, M.H. and Bach, M. (eds), 1994, *Disability is Not Measles: New Research Paradigms in Disability*, Roeher Institute, Ontario, Canada, pp. 181–99.

Figueroa, P., 1993, Equality, Multiculturalism, Antiracism and Physical Education in the National Curriculum, in Evans, J. (ed.), 1993, *Equality, Education and Physical Education*, The Falmer Press, London, pp. 90–104.

Fiji Government Website (http://www.fiji.gov.fj/uploads/FToday2006_2007.doc) accessed 15 October 2008.

Finkelstein, V., 1980, *Attitudes and Disabled People: Issues for Discussion*, monograph 5, World Rehabilitation Fund, New York.

Foucault, M., 1976, *The History of Sexuality: An Introduction*, Penguin, Harmondsworth, UK.

French, R., 1997, *Cerebral Palsy Definition*, on Texas Women's University website (http://venus.teu.edu/~f_huettig/cerebral.htm) accessed 16 March 1999.

French, S., 1993, Disability, Impairment, or Somewhere in Between, in Swain, J., Finkelstein, V., French, S. and Oliver, M. (eds), 1993, *Disabling Barriers – Enabling Environments*, Open University, Milton Keynes, pp. 17–25.

French, S. (ed.), 1994, *On Equal Terms: Working with Disabled People*, Butterworth-Heinemann Ltd, Oxford.

French, J. and Hainsworth, P., 2001, 'There Aren't any Buses and the Swimming Pool's always Cold!': Obstacles and Ppportunities in the Provision of Sport for Disabled People, *Managing Leisure*, Vol. 6(1), 35–49.

Friends of Israel Disabled Veterans website (www.fidv.org/zdvo.html) accessed 15 February 2008.

Gal, J. and Bar, M., 2000, The Needed and the Needy: The Policy Legacies of Benefits for Disabled War Veterans in Israel, *Journal of Social Policy*, Vol. 29(4), p. 577–598.

Gao, C.T. and Liang, S.Y. (2004). *Low Acceptance of Enterprises in Employing People with disabilities*, on *United News* website (http://udn.com/NEWS/LIFE/LIFS1/1978138.shtml) in Huang, C.J., 2005, Discourses of Disability Sport: Experiences of Elite Male and Female Athletes in Britain and Taiwan, Unpublished PhD Thesis, Brunel University, UK.

Girginov, V. and Parry, J., 2005, *The Olympic Games Explained*, Routledge, Abingdon.

GLAD, 1988, *The Impact of Transport on the Quallity of Life and Lifestyles of Young People with Physical Disabilities, Transport Paper No. 2*, Greater London Association for Disabled People, London.

Goodman, S.,1986, *Spirit of Stoke Mandeville: The Story of Sir Ludwig Guttmann*, Collins, London.

Government of Zimbabwe, 1997, *Inter-Censual Demographic Survey*, Harare, Zimbabwe: Author.

Gramsci, A., 1971, *Selections from the Prison Notebooks*, Edited by Greengross, Q. and Nowell Smith, G., Lawrence and Wishart, London.

Green, M. and Houlihan, B., 2005, *Elite Sport Development: Policy Learning and Political Priotries*, Routledge, Abingdon.

Grey-Thompson, Dame T., 2008, *Cheating does Happen in the Paralympics*, (http://www.telegraph.co.uk/sport/othersports/paralympicsport/2798515/Cheating-does-happens-in-the-Paralympics-Paralympics.html) accessed 10 February 2009.

Grimes, P.S. and French, L., 1987, Barriers to Disabled Women's Participation in Sports, *JOPERD*, March 1987, Vol. 58(3), pp. 24–7.

Guthrie, S.R., 1999, Managing Imperfection in a Perfectionist Culture: Physical Activity and Disability Management Among Women with Disabilities, *Quest*, Vol. 51, pp. 369–81.

Guttmann. L., 1952, On the Way to an International Sports Movement for the Paralysed, *The Cord*, Vol. 5 (3) (October), pp. 7–23.

Guttmann, L.,1954, Looking Back on a Decade, *The Cord*, Vol. 6(4), pp. 9–23.

Guttmann, L.,1976, *Textbook of Sport for the Disabled*, HM and M Publishers, Aylesbury.

Hallett, S, 2006a, One eye on China: Back in the People's Republic, *Ouch*, Thursday 26 January (http://www.bbc.co.uk/ouch/features/one-eye-on-china-back.shtml) accessed 28 November 2008.

Hallett, S, 2006b, One eye on China: Mainly for Show, *Ouch*, Thursday 28 February (http://www.bbc.co.uk/ouch/features/one-eye-on-china-mainly-for-show.shtml) accessed 28 November 2008.

Handicap-International Website (http://www.handicap-international.org.uk/page_170.php) accessed 15 October 2008.

Haralambos, M. and Holborn, M., 2000, *Sociology: Themes and Perspectives* (5th edn), Collins, London.

Hardin, M., 2003, Marketing the Acceptably Athletic Image: Wheelchair Athletes, Sport-Related Advertising and Capitalist Hegemony, *Disability Studies Quarterly*, Vol. 23(1), pp. 108–25.

Hardin, B. and Hardin, M., 2003, Conformity and Conflict: Wheelchair Athletes Discuss Sport Media, *Adapted Physical Activity Quarterly*, Vol. 20, pp. 246–59.

Hardin, B. and Hardin, M., 2004, Distorted Pictures: Images of Disability in Physical Education Textbooks, *Adapted Physical Activity Quarterly*, Vol. 21, pp. 399–413.

Hardin, M., Lynn, S. and Walsdorf, K., 2006, Depicting the Sporting Body: The Intersection of Gender, Race and Disability in Women's Sport/Fitness Magazines, *Journal of Magazine and New Media Research*, Vol. 8(1), pp. 1–16.

Hardin, B., Hardin, M., Lynn, S. and Walsdorf, K., 2001, Missing in Action? Images of Disability in Sports Illustrated for Kids, *Disability Studies Quarterly*, Vol. 21(2).

Hargreaves, J., 2000, *Heroines of Sport: The Politics of Difference and Identity*, Routledge, London.

Harris, P., 1994, Self-induced autonomic dysreflexia ('boosting') practised by some tetraplegic athletes to enhance their athletic performance, *Paraplegia*, Vol. 32(5), pp. 289–91.

Hehir, T., 2002, Eliminating Ableism in Education, *The Harvard Educational Review*, Spring 2002, Vol. 72(1), pp.1–32.

Hinds, D., 1951, Alice at the Paralympiad, *The Cord*, Vol. 4(1), pp. 27–32.

Hogan, A., 1999, Carving out a space to act: acquired impairment and contested identity, in Corker, M, and French, S.(eds), 1999, *Disability Discourse*, Open University Press, Buckingham, UK, pp. 79–91.

Howe, P.D., 2008, *The Cultural Politics of the Paralympic Movement: Through an Anthropological Lens*, Routledge, London.

Howe, P.D. and Jones, C., 2006, Classification of Disabled Athletes: (Dis)Empowering the Paralympic Practice Community, *Sociology of Sport Journal*, Vol. 23, pp. 29–46.

Huang, C.J., 2005, Discourses of Disability Sport: Experiences of Elite Male and Female Athletes in Britain and Taiwan, Unpublished PhD Thesis, Brunel University, UK.

Hums, M., Moorman, A.M. and Wolff, E.A., 2003, The Inclusion of the Paralympics in the Olympic and Amateur Sports Act, *Journal of Sport and Social Issues*, Vol. 27(3), pp. 261–75.

Hunt, P. (ed.), 1966, *Stigma: The Experience of Disability*, Chapman, London.

Hylton, K. and Bramham, P.(eds), 2008, *Sports Development: Policy Process and Practice*, Routledge, Abingdon, UK.

Imrie, R., *Rethinking the Relationships between Disability, Rehabilitation, and Society, Disability and Rehabilitation*, 1997, Vol. 19, No. 7, pp. 263–71.

International Paralympic Committee, 2006, *IPC Strategic Plan 2006–2009*, IPC, Bonn, Germany.

International Paralympic Committee Website, 2009a, IPC General Structure, (http://www.paralympic.org/release/Main_Sections_Menu/IPC/Organization/)   accessed 10 February 2009.

International Paralympic Committee Website, 2009b, *IPC Annual Reports 2004–2007*, (http://www.paralympic.org/release/Main_Sections_Menu/IPC/Reference_Documents/) accessed 10 February 2009.

International Paralympic Committee Website, 2009c, *Vision and Mission*, (http://www.paralympic.org/release/Main_Sections_Menu/IPC/About_the_IPC/Vision_and_Mission/) accessed 10 February 2009.

International Paralympic Committee Website, 2009d, *Paralympian Ambassadors*, (http://www.paralympic.org/release/Main_Sections_Menu/Partners_and_Patrons/Paralylmpian_Ambassadors/index.html) accessed 10 February 2009.

International Paralympic Committee Website, 2009e, *IPC Honorary Board*, (http://www.paralympic.org/release/Main_Sections_Menu/Partners_and_Patrons/Honorary_Board/index.html) accessed 10 February 2009.

International Paralympic Committee Website, 2009[6], *New Russian Law Upholds Paralympic Standards*, (http://www.paralympic.org/release/Main_Sections_Menu/News/Current_Affairs/2008_11_07_a.html) accessed 10 February 2009.

International Paralympic Committee Website, 2009f, *Organizational Development Initiative*, (http://www.paralympic.org/release/Main_Sections_Menu/Development/ODI/index.html) accessed 10 February 2009.

International Paralympic Committee Website, 2009g, *Joint Statement on the Re-inclusion of Athletes With Intellectual Disability in Future Paralympic Games*, (http://www.paralympic.org/release/Main_Sections_Menu/News/Current_Affairs/2008_09_13_a.html) accessed 10 February 2009.

IPC Newsletter, 2001a, The New IPC Symbol, Vol 2(1), p.1.

IPC Newsletter, 2001b, What is the status of the IPC Symbol??, Vol. 2(2), p.1.

IPC Strategic Plan, 2006 (http://www.paralympic.org/release/Main_Sections_Menu/IPC/Reference_Documents/), accessed 28 November 2008.

IPC, 2008; Personal Communication. Excerpt from AHSN handbook emailed 2 December 2008 (unpaginated).

Israel21c website (http://www.israel21c.org/bin/en.jsp?enDisplay=view&enDispWh at=object&enZone=Culture&enDispWho=Articles%5El785&enPage=BlankP age) accessed 15 February 2008.

Jarvie, G., 2006, *Sport, Culture and Society: An Introduction*, Routledge, Abingdon.

Kew, F., 1997, *Sport: Social Problems and Issues*, Butterworth Heinemann, Oxford.

Kolkka, T. and Williams, T., 1997, Gender and Disability Sport Participation: Setting a Sociological Research Agenda, *Adapted Physical Activity Quarterly*, Vol. 14, pp. 8–23.

Kuao, L.H., 2001, Taiwanese Women's Right White Paper. Taiwanese Women Employment Facilitating Association in Huang, C.J., 2005, Discourses of Disability Sport: [BL], Unpublished PhD Thesis, Brunel University, UK.

Labanowich, S.,1989, The Paralympic Games: A Retrospective View, *Palaestra*, Summer 1989.

Layder, D., 1994, *Understanding Social Theory*, Sage, London.

Legg, D., Emes, C., Stewart, D. and Steadward, R, 2002, Historical Overview of the Paralympics, Special Olympics and Deaflympics, *Palaestra*, 20.1 (Winter 2002), pp. 30–35, 56.

Lepore, M., Gayle, G.W. and Stevens, S., 2007, *Adapted Aquatics Programming: A Professional Guide*, Human Kinetics, London.

Lockwood, R. and Lockwood, A., 2007, *Rolling Back The Years: A History of Wheelchair Sports in Western Australia*, Wheelchair Sports, WA Inc; Perth, Australia.

Lomi, C., Geroulanos, E. and Kekatos, E., 2004, Sir Ludwig Guttmann – 'The de Coubertin of the Paralysed', 2004, *Journal of the Hellenic Association of Orthopaedics and Traumatology*, Vol, 55 (1). (http://www.acta-ortho.gr/v55t1_6.html) accessed 7 November 2008.

Lonsdale, S., 1990, *Women with Disabilities: The Experience of Physical Disability among Women*, Macmillan Education, London.

Loveandpiste Website, 2008, History of Skiing, (http://www.loveandpiste.co.uk/historyofskiing.php) accessed 21 October 2008.

Lukes, S., 1974, *Power: A Radical View*, Macmillan, London.

McCann, C., 1996, Sports for the Disabled: the evolution from rehabilitation to competitive sport, *British Journal of Sports Medicine*, Vol. 30(4), pp. 279–80.

MacClancey, J. (ed.), 1996, *Sport, Identity and Ethnicity*, Berg, Oxford.

Maharaj, 2008; Personal Communication. Email from Dr Jagdish Maharaj dated 23 June 2008.

Malanga, G.A., 2008, *Athletes with Disabilities*, (http://www.emedicine.com/sports/TOPIC144.HTM) accessed 20 November 2008.

Mastro, J.V., Hall, M.M., and Canabal, M.Y., 1988, Cultural and Attitudinal Similarities – Females and Disabled Individuals in Sports and Athletics, *JOPERD*, Nov/Dec 1988, Vol. 59(9), pp. 80–3.

Middleton, L., 1999, *Disabled Children: Challenging Social Exclusion*, Blackwell Science, Oxford.

Morris, J., 1991, *Pride Against Prejudice: Transforming Attitudes to Disability*, The Women's Press Ltd, London.

Morris, J., 1993, Prejudice in Swain, J., Finkelstein, V., French, S. and Oliver, M. (eds), 1993, *Disabling Barriers – Enabling Environments*, Open University, Milton Keynes.

Morris, J., 1996, Introduction, in Morris, J. (ed.), *Encounters with Strangers: Feminism and Disability*, The Women's Free Press, London, UK, pp. 1–12.

Mpofu, E. and Harley, D.A., 2002, Disability and Rehabilitation in Zimbabwe: Lessons and Implications for Rehabilitation Practice in the US – Disability and Rehabilitation in Zimbabwe, *Journal of Rehabilitation* (http://findarticles.com/p/articles/mi_m0825/is_/ai_95105818) accessed 20 October 2008.

Nash, E., 2001, We Are Not the Champions, *The Independent* 22 July 2001 (http://findarticles.com/p/articles/mi_qn4158/is_20010722/ai_n14409753/pg_1?tag=artBody;col1) accessed 7 November 2008.

National Institute of Statistics (NIS), 2003, *Statistical Yearbook*, National Institute of Statistics, Phnom Penh.

Neale, C., 2000, Comments on BBC Sport website (http://news.bbc.co.uk/sport/hi/english/sports_talk/newsid_988000/988174.stm) accessed 7 November 2008.

Northern Officer Group, 1996, The Disability Discrimination Act: a policy and practice guide for local government, Northern Officer Group, Wakefield.

O'Donnell, M., 1997, *Introduction to Sociology* (4th edn), Thomas Nelson and Sons Ltd, Walton on Thames.

Olenik, L.M., 1998, Women in Elite Disability Sport: Multidimensional Perspectives, Unpublished PhD Thesis, University of Alberta, Edmonton, Canada.

Oliver, M., 1993a, Disability and Dependency: A Creation of Industrial Societies? in Swain, J., Finkelstein, V., French, S. and Oliver, M. (eds), 1993, *Disabling Barriers – Enabling Environments*, Open University, Milton Keynes, pp. 49–60.

Oliver, M.,1993b, Re-defining Disability: A Challenge to Research in Swain, J., Finkelstein, V., French, S. and Oliver, M. (eds), 1993, *Disabling Barriers – Enabling Environments*, Open University, Milton Keynes, pp. 61–8.

Oliver, M., 1996, *Understanding Disability: From Theory to Practice*, Macmillan Press Ltd, London.

Oxford Illustrated Dictionary, 1998, Oxford University Press, Oxford.

Pappous, A., 2008, The Photographic Coverage of the Paralympic Games, Paper presented at the Third Annual International Forum on Children with Special Needs "Sport and Ability", Shafallah Centre, Doha, Qatar, 20–22 April, 2008.

The Paralympian, 2001, IPC Investigation Commission Finds Two-Thirds of INAS-FID Forms to be Invalid, No. 1, p. 2.

The Paralympian, 2002, Paralympic Games/Salt Lake City, No. 2, p. 2.

Pickering Francis, L., 2005, Competitive Sports, Disability, and Problems of Justice in Sports, *Journal of the Philosophy of Sport*, Vol. 32, pp. 127–32.

Priestley, M., 1998, Constructions and Creations: Idealism, Materialism and Disability Theory, *Disability and Society*, Vol. 13(1), pp.75–94.

Quinn, N., 2007, The Representation of Disability by the Canadian Broadcasting Corporation (CBC) during the 2004 Summer Paralympic Games, Unpublished Masters Thesis, University of Toronto, Canada.

Regent, 2008; Personal Communication. Email from Rob Regent dated 14 June 2008.

Reiser, R. and Mason, M., 1990, *Disability Equality in the Classroom: A Human Rights Issue*, Inner London Education Authority, London.

Reuters Health, 2008, *Minorities with Disabilities Suffer Most* (http://www.reuters.com/article/healthNews/idUSTRE4926FE20081003) accessed 20 October 2008.

Sainsbury, T., 1998, The Paralympic Movement, Paper presented at the British Olympic Academy, Wembley Hilton Hotel, London.

Schäfer 2008; Personal Communication. Email from Alexis Schäfer, 27 September 2008.

Schantz, O.J. and Gilbert, K., 2001, An Ideal Misconstrued: Newspaper Coverage of the Atlanta Paralympic Games in France and Germany, *Sociology of Sport Journal*, Vol. 18, pp. 69–94.

Schell, L.A.B. and Duncan, M.C., 1999, A Content Analysis of CBS's Coverage of the 1996 Paralympic Games, *Adapted Physical Activity Quarterly*, Vol. 16, pp. 27–47.

Schmeckl, 2008; Personal Communication. Email from Jörg Schmeckl, 21 September 2008

Schreiner, P. and Strohkendl, H., 2006, The Disappearance of Athletes with Severe Disabilities in Wheelchair Rugby, Paper presented at the Vista 2006 Conference entitled 'Classification: Solutions for the Future' held in Bonn, Germany, 6–7 May, 2006.

Schwartz, A., 2008, *Paralympic Athletes Add Equality to Their Goals* (http://www.nytimes.com/2008/09/06/sports/othersports/06paralympics.html?_r=3&hp=&oref=slogin&pagewanted=print&oref=slogin) accessed 21 October 2008.

Scruton, J., 1956, International Stoke Mandeville Games, *The Cord*, Vol. 8(4), pp. 7–21.

Scruton, J., 1957, The 1957 International Stoke Mandeville Games, *The Cord*, Vol. 9(4), pp. 7–28.

Scruton, J., 1964, History of Sport for the Paralysed, *The Cord*, Vol. 17 (1).

Scruton, J., 1998, *Stoke Mandeville: Road to the Paralympics*, The Peterhouse Press, Aylesbury.

Seymour, W., 1989, *Body Alterations*, Unwin Hyman, London.

Shakespeare, T. and Watson, N.,1997, Defending the Social Model, *Disability and Society*, Vol.12, No. 2, pp. 293–300.

Shearer, A., 1981, *Disability: Whose Handicap?*, Basil Blackwell, Oxford.

Sherrill, C. (ed.), 1986, *Sport and Disabled Athletes*, Champaign, Il., Human Kinetics, London.

Sherrill, C., 1993, Women with Disability, Paralympics and Reasoned Action Contact Theory, *Women in Sport and Physical Activity Journal*, Vol. 2(2), pp. 51–60.

Sherrill, C., 1997, Paralympic Games 1996: Feminist and Other Concerns: What's Your Excuse?, *Palaestra*, Winter; pp. 32–8.

Shved, M., 2005, Adapted Physical Activity in Israel, Online Masters Thesis (Overview), (http://www.kuleuven.be/emdapa/comparative/Israel.pdf) accessed 15 February 2008.

Smith, A. and Twomey, B., 2002, Labour Market Experiences of People with Disabilities. *Labour Market Trends*, August, 110(8), pp. 41–427 (http://www.statistics.gov.uk/articles/labour_market_trends/People_with_disabilities_aug2002.pdf) accessed 7 November 2008.

Southam, M., 1994, Sport, Leisure, Disability, *The Leisure Manager*, Oct/Nov 1994, pp. 12–14.

Special Olympics International Website (http://www.specialolympics.org) accessed 28 November 2008.

Speedski Website, 2008, *History of Alpine Skiing*, (http://www.speedski.com/HistoryofSkiing.htm) accessed 21 October 2008.

Sport England, 2001, *Disability Survey 2000: Young People with a Disability and Sport – Headline Findings*, Sport England, London.

Statistics Norway Website, 2008, *From Cradle to Grave: Growing Number of Disability Pensioners*, (http://www.ssb.no/norge_en/omsorg_en.pdf) accessed 21 October 2008.

Steadward, R.D., 1992, Excellence – The Future of Sports for Athletes with Disabilities, in Williams, T., Almond, L. and Sparkes, A. (eds), 1992, *Sport and Physical Activity: Moving Towards Excellence*, E and FN Spon, London, pp. 293–99.

Stein, J.U., 1989, U.S. Media – Where Were You During 1988 Paralympics?, *Palaestra*, Summer, pp. 45–52.

Stone, E., 2001, Disability, Sport and the Body in China, *Sociology of Sport Journal*, 18, pp. 51–68.

Swain, J., Finkelstein, V., French, S. and Oliver, M. (eds), 1993, *Disabling Barriers – Enabling Environments*, Open University, Milton Keynes.

Swartz, L., and Watermeyer, B., 2008, Cyborg Anxiety: Oscar Pistorius and the Boundaries of What it Means to be Human, *Disability and Society*, Vol. 23(2), pp. 187–90.

Taiwan Federation of the Disabled, 2001, Life Circumstances Report of People With Disabilities in 2001. (http://www.enable.org.tw/res/res2001.htm) accessed 15 September 2004 in Huang, C.J., 2005, Discourses of Disability Sport: Experiences of Elite Male and Female Athletes in Britain and Taiwan, Unpublished PhD Thesis, Brunel University, UK.

Tang Yuankai, 2004, *Taking on Fate: Disabled Chinese in Sports*, (http://www.bjreview.com.cn/200443/Nation-200443(B).htm) accessed 28 July 2006.

Thierfeld, J. and Gibbons, G., 1986, From Access to Equity: Opening Doors for Women Athletes, *Sports n Spokes*, May/June 1986, pp. 21–23.

Thomas, N. and Smith, A., 2003, Preoccupied with Able-Bodiedness? An Analysis of the British Media Coverage of the 2000 Paralympic Games. *Physical Activity Quarterly*, Vol. 20, pp. 166–81.

Tiemann, H., 1999, Exploring the Sporting Lives of Women With a Physical Disability, in Doll-Tepper, G., Kroener, M. and Sonnenschein, W. (eds), 2001, *New Horizons in Sport for Athletes with a Disability: proceedings of the International Vista '99 Conference*, Vol. 2, Meyer and Meyer Sport (UK) Ltd, Oxford, pp. 643–54.

Tomlinson, A. (ed.), 2007, *The Sports Studies Reader*, Routledge, Abingdon.

UK Sport, 2000, *United Kingdom's Sporting Preferences*, UK Sport, London.

Union of Physically Impaired Against Segregation (UPIAS), 1976, *Fundamental Principles of Disability*, UPIAS, London.

United Nations Statistics Division, 2006, *Demographic Yearbook – Table 3: Population by Sex, Rate of Population Increase, Surface Area and Density* (http://unstats.un.org/unsd/demographic/products/dyb/dyb2006/Table03.pdf) accessed 15 October 2008.

Webster's Third New International Dictionaryof the English Language Unabridged, 1961, Merriam-Webster Inc., Publishers, Springfield, MA.

Wendell, S., 1996, *The Rejected Body: Feminist Phiolosophical Reflections on Disability*, Routledge, London.

Wilhite, B., 2002, *Sport for Athletes with Severe Disabilities – Identifying Key Issues Affecting the Future of Disability and Sport.* (http://www.europaralympic.org/doping/Bratislava/hosts.htm) accessed 10 February 2009.

Wolbring, G., 2008, Oscar Pistorious and the Future Nature of Olympic, Paralympic and other Sports, *Scripted*, Vol. 5(1), pp. 139–60.

World Health Organisation (1980) in DePauw, K.P., 1997, The (In)Visibility of DisAbility: Cultural Contexts and "Sporting Bodies" in Quest, November 1997, Vol. 49 (4), p. 422.

VII World Wheelchair Games Final Report, 1984, Part 2, Appendix A.

Zahal Disabled Veterans Organisation website (http://zdvo.org/zdvo.html) accessed 15 February 2008.

Index